W9-BZA-331

DEADLY INDIFFERENCE

DEADLY INDIFFERENCE

THE PERFECT (POLITICAL) STORM
HURRICANE KATRINA, THE BUSH WHITE HOUSE, AND BEYOND

MICHAEL D. BROWN
and TED SCHWARZ

TAYLOR TRADE PUBLISHING
Lanham • New York • Boulder • Toronto • Plymouth, UK

Published by Taylor Trade Publishing
An imprint of The Rowman & Littlefield Publishing Group, Inc.
4501 Forbes Boulevard, Suite 200, Lanham, Maryland 20706
http://www.rlpgtrade.com

Estover Road, Plymouth PL6 7PY, United Kingdom

Distributed by National Book Network

Copyright © 2011 by Michael D. Brown and Ted Schwarz

All rights reserved. No part of this book may be reproduced in any form or by any electronic or mechanical means, including information storage and retrieval systems, without
written permission from the publisher, except by a reviewer who may quote passages in a
review.

British Library Cataloguing in Publication Information Available

Library of Congress Cataloging-in-Publication Data
Brown, Michael D. (Michael DeWayne), 1954–
    Deadly indifference : the perfect (political) storm : Hurricane Katrina, the Bush White
House, and beyond / Michael D. Brown and Ted Schwarz.
        p. cm.
    Includes index.
    ISBN 978-1-58979-485-6 (cloth : alk. paper) — ISBN 978-1-58979-486-3 (electronic)
    1. Hurricane Katrina, 2005. 2. Brown, Michael D. (Michael DeWayne), 1954–
3. United States. Federal Emergency Management Agency—Officials and employees—
Biography. 4. Disaster relief—Government policy—Gulf Coast (U.S.)—History—
21st century. 5. Disaster relief—Government policy—Louisiana—New Orleans—
History—21st century. 6. Disaster relief—Government policy—United States—
History—21st century. 7. Emergency management—United States—History—
21st century. 8. United States—Politics and government—2001–2009. 9. Mass media—
Political aspects—United States—History—21st century. 10. Apathy—Political
aspects—United States—History—21st century. I. Schwarz, Ted, 1945– II. Title.
HV636 2005 .G85 B76 2011
976'.044—dc22   2011004549

∞™ The paper used in this publication meets the minimum requirements of American
National Standard for Information Sciences—Permanence of Paper for Printed Library
Materials, ANSI/NISO Z39.48-1992.

Printed in the United States of America

CONTENTS

CHAPTER 1

WELCOME TO D.C.

THE FIRST LESSON I learned when President George W. Bush appointed me Under Secretary of Homeland Security was that few people understood the concept of what I have come to call *deadly indifference*, and almost no one wanted to deal with its many realities.

The people of the United States accept that we need a strong defense that includes intelligence gathering, which could prevent another 9/11. We support the development of ever more sophisticated weapons; well-trained, well-equipped armed forces; close ties with the friendly countries to the immediate north and south of us; and a powerful Coast Guard protecting our coastlines.

We accept the need to respond to health issues, such as an impending influenza pandemic, with whatever vaccines might prevent the illness or save the lives of those with the most severe conditions. And those who live in areas where natural disasters—hurricanes, tornadoes, floods, mudslides, and earthquakes—are regular, albeit often unpredictable, occurrences recognize the need to be able to respond quickly to the needs of those in danger.

INDIFFERENCE AND DENIAL

Other concerns are ignored for one reason or another: budget constraints that reduce spending without regard for critical need, bias against the socioeconomic level of the people affected, the desire to look prepared for a disaster rather than face criticism for admitting we're not, and refusing to take what will be an unpopular stand even though it is the right thing to do.

There is also a denial of what constitutes danger to one's self or one's community. The city of Los Angeles is concerned with how emergency services can respond to the next earthquake, knowing that both small and large quakes are a relatively unpredictable but certain aspect of living in the region. And while Los Angeles—and California—take earthquake planning seriously, in the midst of a major earthquake, most services will be lost, communications limited, and frustrated clusters of populations left isolated, shocked, and disoriented. Yet this does not change the fact that every year thousands of people move into earthquake-prone neighborhoods. These newcomers are indifferent to the risk, and unless something shocks them into facing reality, they ignore what should be their first concern.

For example, a former television executive—an attorney and executive producer—quit her job and moved east within a few weeks of her daughter starting kindergarten. As is common throughout the country, the parents of these schoolchildren were expected to provide certain supplies that might be needed during the school year. These included a box of tissues, a container of hand sanitizer, crayons, an old shirt to use as a smock when painting, and an earthquake kit containing some food and a letter assuring her daughter that she would pick her up as soon as possible. The list was given without explanation, as though a child taking his or her own earthquake kit to school was a normal occurrence.

It was a normal occurrence, of course, but not if you were indifferent to the realities of a very dangerous region of the country. The producer finally understood that all the jokes about "the big one" had such a harsh basis in fact that no job, no weather conditions, and no home was worth the possible loss of a child.

Similar stories can be told of people moving to hurricane-prone Florida or tornado-prone Oklahoma or flood-prone Iowa or blizzard-prone Minnesota or any of the wildfire-prone states. Virtually everywhere we live presents us with hazards and potential disasters that we choose to overlook, instead seeing only the beauty of the coasts, the majesty of the mountains, or the magnificence of the rivers.

The specifics of this problem vary from community to community, state to state, and nation to nation, but they exist without regard to politics, citizenship, or theology. In fact, for some, the causes might be lumped together under the acronym of NIMBI— Not In *My* Best Interest. NIMBI did not cause Hurricane Katrina, America's deadliest natural disaster in recent years. But lives were lost, and hardworking individuals were ridiculed, ignored, and then blamed for failing at a task those responsible would not allow to be handled in a timely manner. And having been the person most responsible for coordinating the federal government's preparation for the coming storm and its role in the aftermath, I had a unique view of what might be called the perfect political storm. Local leaders delayed acting to avoid voter backlash in case events changed at the last minute and constituents questioned their decisions; state leaders with exhausted regional resources tried to take credit for whatever worked while blaming others for any failures; members of Congress pretended that photo ops at the disaster site actually meant they were involved with recovery; and the agencies truly involved attempted to accomplish a job where their success would be attributed to others. Votes would be gained and lost, a situation that many in Washington saw as being of far greater concern than a hurricane whose destructive force had passed. It was a perfect political storm that would one day make or break careers, including mine.

Hurricane Katrina happened during a Republican administration, but the harsh realities transcend political parties, economics, age, race, or ethnic origins. In one form or another, we are too often a nation in denial.

This is not to say that most people fail to recognize inherent dangers where they choose to live. They consider their lifestyle choices to be ones where they recognize potential dangers but feel they are worth the risks. Where I lived in Colorado, fire prevention efforts on your property—fire-retardant shingles, carefully positioned water hoses, clearing of ground cover, and planned escape routes—become the trade-off one makes for living in the midst of the natural beauty.

In other locations around the country, the construction of breakwaters and other protective barriers becomes the trade-off for living near the water's edge. People realize there is a risk, a downside to experiencing what they consider great beauty all around them, and most plan how to handle whatever might go wrong. This is no different from moving into an urban high-rise apartment in a high-crime area, delighting in the view, the ability to walk to work, to get around by bicycle more than car, and so forth, but adding high-security locks and an alarm system.

However, it is inexcusable when developers, politicians, and others with a vested interest in an unsafe location—a so-called hundred-year floodplain, for example—pretend they know the short- and long-term safety of the area. They sell commercial property as though the dangers and their timing are predictable, vilifying those who say otherwise.

When a professor at Arizona State University in Tempe stated that removing groundwater from a suburb popular with developers was a danger to the community, he was told he was wrong. More and more houses were built without problems . . . until sinkholes developed randomly, essentially swallowing yards, rendering buildings unsafe, and causing other damage. All of us make lifestyle choices, sometimes recognizing what we are doing and the price we may pay, but sometimes we are misled by elected officials and unscrupulous businesspeople who sell a dream of the moment without mentioning the likely nightmare in the years to come.

* * *

Personal journal entry, October 12, 2001, one month after terrorists attacked the World Trade Towers and the Pentagon:

> *The Consequence Management Working Group is to identify holes or defects in our consequence management assets and strategies. We are to identify areas where we're weak in responding to a terrorist attack and how we can respond better in the future.*
>
> *The CMWG initially utilized the FEMA Emergency Support Teams [EST] that were already . . . coordinating the response to the New York and Pentagon attacks. The group identified a large hole in our ability to respond to biological or chemical attacks. The group . . . determined that our vaccine and pharmaceutical stockpiles were inadequate, including equipment to disperse the drugs. They also identified holes in the equipment and protective*

equipment available to first responders and others who would respond to such an incident.

The CMWG also reviewed the entire Federal Response Plan and identified 137 different deficiencies that needed to be corrected.

The same day that I was a part of the briefing given at the White House to President George W. Bush, Vice President Dick Cheney, Defense Secretary Donald Rumsfeld, Secretary of State Colin Powell, and other high officials, a simultaneous briefing on the same subject was being given to Congress. Both briefings were based on the same material, but as I noted in my journal:

The briefing created a stir, because while we were busy telling the President that we weren't ready for a chem/bio attack, Secretary of Health and Human Services Tommy Thompson was testifying on the Hill that essentially we were completely ready for such an attack. Of course his testimony made all the headlines at the same time the President was being told the opposite. On the next NSC [National Security Council] Deputies' conference call the Assistant Secretary of HHS, Claude Allen, told the group the same thing. I sat in stunned silence. . . . Certainly HHS had identified the same issues we had, and were trying to get programs and money in place to address these concerns. However, it was clear we still weren't prepared for a chem/bio attack.

That was my thinking in those early weeks as under secretary. Like perhaps most people in the United States, I developed a feeling of insularity. We were being attacked by people from other countries, other cultures, other belief systems. We had experienced a first strike with more than three thousand deaths that revealed the nation's largest city to be vulnerable to isolation. People fled on foot across bridges and through tunnels. But Manhattan could have been totally isolated if all escape routes had been cut off, either by an enemy or by panic. The island city had been lucky as well as unfortunate, and I, like many others in government and private think tanks, at first felt we had to plan better and be ready for the next assault. I felt comfortable with the government rhetoric—the need to destroy the enemy before the enemy could return to our soil.

My work as under secretary was actually my second federal government position related to natural and manmade disasters. My first job for President George W. Bush was as general counsel for FEMA— the Federal Emergency Management Agency.

I often describe FEMA's primary role as being the honest broker within the federal government. First, it is an organization that has two things that are critical when there is a regional or national emergency— direct access to the White House and a budget meant to be tapped during crises. All that is necessary to utilize FEMA is for the President to declare an area a federal disaster, after which the agency arranges whatever assistance is needed.

Most Americans think of disasters as relatively infrequent events. They remember 9/11. They remember one or two hurricanes or a tornado cutting a swath of destruction through the Midwest. By the time I was preparing for Hurricane Katrina at the start of George W. Bush's second term, I had been responsible for the federal response to 160 different presidentially declared disasters.

FEMA originally was considered the agency that would handle the federal response to disasters. That was in 1979. Jimmy Carter was president, and though he was already having problems in the Middle East, no one expected the United States to be attacked in the manner of 9/11. That thinking changed under President Ronald Reagan, who was concerned with a Soviet attack and the domestic needs for running the government when the country had been struck by atomic weapons, again something that was feared but which didn't happen. The idea of a natural disaster gradually faded for the planning personnel to such a degree that just ten years after its creation for such eventualities, FEMA was unable to handle hurricane damage.

It was under President Bill Clinton that FEMA, then led by James Lee Witt, entered a stage I thought it should have been at all along. This was the planning for all hazards facing the country, whether natural or manmade. The idea, in its simplest form, means that it doesn't matter what causes a building to fall, a bridge to collapse, or any other catastrophe. The rescue of trapped survivors, cleanup, and restoration concerns are the same. FEMA would be ready for whatever might occur, whether it was caused by Mother Nature or man.

By the time I became involved with FEMA, the 9/11 attack had caused many in Congress to return to the idea that FEMA should be a part of the antiterrorism effort. Suddenly there was less flexibility, fewer options for response. In addition, while the Department of Homeland Security had 180,000 employees, FEMA had fewer than 1,700 men and women. The bastardization of FEMA's mission, the evisceration of its budget, and the shifting of its personnel, had created an air of tension, disillusionment, and distrust of the administration's reorganization plans. However, everyone in FEMA continued to be as effective as possible each time we were needed.

When FEMA made a request during a disaster or crisis, several things happened. First, if an agency such as the Department of Transportation was tasked by FEMA to do something, their action would show the agency, its personnel, and its leadership in a beneficial light. The media would cover what was happening with positive stories about tax dollars flowing from a compassionate government's elected officials and bureaucrats. Even more important to the leadership of a department tasked by FEMA was that the cost of whatever was requested did not come out of their budget. Any costs were reimbursed by FEMA's disaster relief fund budget.

A second role for FEMA, when I became general counsel, was leading the federal government's Continuity of Operations, known as COOP, and its Continuity of Government, known as COG. You may have seen or heard the acronyms, though usually without explanation. The truth is that the two responsibilities were among the most important, most challenging, and, to be honest, some of the coolest activities I could imagine.

Continuity of Operations was established in case the operations of the federal government were disrupted in some way. FEMA was the agency that had the facilities, the procedures, the money, and the other means to keep the government operating in a new, safe location.

The classic example is a disaster happening in Washington, D.C. While most people think of an enemy attack on the city, natural disasters are often the greatest threat. For example, in September 2003,

Hurricane Isabel was headed for the nation's capital. We had no idea if it would strike and certainly no sense of how strong it would be when it reached land. What we did know was that if the worst-case scenario occurred, government operations would be disrupted.

FEMA had no idea how the crisis would be handled by the state and local governments in the District of Columbia, Virginia, and Maryland, nor was it our job to order an evacuation or otherwise give orders in that regard. Our job was to maintain parallel government operations in a location safe from possible disaster. Should Washington, D.C., be temporarily shut down by the hurricane, the secondary location would maintain business as usual.

FEMA was, and is, often the subject of conspiracy theorists because of its Continuity of Operations and Continuity of Government roles. One such theory was that FEMA was the shadow government, the hidden force that really ran the country. According to some conspiracy theorists, FEMA could declare martial law and take control of the nation.

For Hurricane Isabel, the D.C. government never bothered to order an evacuation. District officials issued warnings concerning the force of the storm and the potential danger, but that was the extent of it. However, FEMA alerted every government department and agency to implement their COOP plan. This meant that designated teams of employees were immediately sent from each agency to whatever facility had been delegated for their use. They would then prepare to continue the agency's work should D.C. be temporarily shut down.

Some of the facilities were in regions in no danger from whatever was happening in Washington. Some of the locations were underground, such as Mt. Weather in Virginia, one of the sexy "black ops" types of places that really exist but, in part, had no different purpose than any of the aboveground facilities. Once in position and the distant offices readied for immediate operation, the teams would simply wait. Rarely were they needed, but they always had to be prepared.

* * *

Journal entry from September 26, 2003:

> *Shortly after the hurricane hit, John Gordon called and told me that the White House was going to want me to brief the*

President on the status of our response to Hurricane Isabel. It was primarily a photo opportunity to convey that the President was concerned about our efforts . . .

* * *

FEMA's most important role is not when something happens. It is when the COOP plan is being devised. FEMA helps with site selection, facility preparation, and equipment testing, and returns again and again to ensure that everything will function as needed in a crisis.

What I found fascinating was the diversity of needs and planning among the various departments and agencies. COOP planning and preparation is done for all branches of government, including both houses of Congress, the Supreme Court, and the White House. We were not in charge of their COOP plans, but we were the liaisons with architects, engineers, construction personnel, real estate personnel, security, and everything else that might be involved. We did whatever they requested and made certain it would function as planned in any emergency. However, we had no involvement in running these distant locations when they were in use, no armed force that could keep citizens in line (whatever that theory meant), and posed none of the fantasy dangers created in the minds of conspiracy buffs.

The idea behind the COOP plans came from the Cold War when Americans were certain that an attack by the Soviet Union was imminent. Approximately fifty years passed before a meaningful danger— the attack on September 11, 2001—tested the planning we had done, but FEMA, formally created in 1979, always functioned as though a crisis was imminent and the nation's leaders had to be prepared.

The Continuity of Government program was the sexier of the two, though some locations served both entities. This is where we had the alternate center of operations for the President of the United States, the alternate communication systems, alternate locations for the Supreme Court and Congress as well as the special communication needs for them. It was COG that arranged for alternate court houses for the Supreme Court, alternate law libraries for their use, and the like. All of this was predicated on the idea, probably first discussed after the Soviet Union exploded a nuclear weapon in 1949, that Washington, D.C., would be destroyed and there had to be a way to keep America functioning. Back then all the thinking was about protective underground bunkers, and FEMA's work was based on the same scenario concerns.

Most Americans do not know that for any event that brings the President and Congress together COG planning takes place. As I write this there has just been a State of the Union Address by the President. It is delivered to both houses of Congress and televised to the nation. Everything seems normal and security appears to be limited to the Secret Service's Presidential Protection division. However, behind the scenes something else is happening without the public's awareness.

One cabinet member never attends the President's speech. Instead, that cabinet member, along with his or her staff, is taken to a secret, undisclosed location. He or she is provided with a communication device known as a Central Locator System. It is identical to one that the President carries so that we know where the President is at all times. In addition, representatives of all departments and agencies of the government are brought to the same place to wait with the cabinet member. If the capital is attacked and we lose the President, the Senate, the House, and the Supreme Court, we have a location from which the people inside can communicate with the rest of the government, communicate with everyone in the United States through the Emergency Broadcast System, and become, in effect, the new seat of government.

I often joked that there were two advantages to being the cabinet person chosen to be away from D.C. One was that he or she got to miss the speech, which could be boring, depending upon the President giving it. And the second was that the food was wonderful. The kitchen in the undisclosed location was staffed with cooks from the White House mess, masters who make meals as good as or better than you find in the best restaurants.

The general counsel's job is to understand all the laws, rules, and policies for everything FEMA does. I had to involve myself with all aspects of running the United States government both when it was functioning normally and when it was dealing with a crisis or in the midst of a crisis. It was a practical and legal education few people, no matter how well educated in government affairs, ever receive.

The reason I came to the attention of the President in the first place was my connection with Joe Allbaugh, probably the least known of the three people comprising the Iron Triangle—Karl Rove, Karen

Hughes, and Joe Allbaugh. Allbaugh was a longtime friend from my college days when, though we went to different schools at different times, we were both active in young Republican politics. [Later, when I was made the scapegoat for the administration in the midst of Katrina, *Time* magazine ran an article claiming I was Joe's college roommate. But I had finished school and was married, and I can assure you that neither my bride nor I had any interest in sharing Joe's dormitory room.]

Joe had been campaign manager when George Bush won the governor's race in Texas and was again involved with the presidential campaign. Karl was the political strategist for the campaigns, and Karen handled communications.

I don't know the details of the history concerning what happened in the formative days of the new administration, but Karen and Karl were given offices within the White House, while Joe was made the director of FEMA, breaking up the Iron Triangle. I knew that Joe had been interested in being chief of staff or working in the West Wing, though what the change meant, I have no idea. Nor did it matter. I was asked by Joe and the White House to be general counsel for FEMA in Washington, D.C. It was the start of an unexpected, sometimes richly rewarding, sometimes rather frightening, education.

FEMA's budget and constant presence in ongoing disasters around the country, plus its regional operations spanning all fifty states, ensured that the agency would be regularly called upon by the White House to help with one activity or another unrelated directly to disasters. Often Joe would be called to see if FEMA could handle the arrangements, covering the costs in order to save the other agency or the White House the money. He, in turn, would usually say no, something I never understood. So long as the request was within our budget and the action we were asked to take was within the mandate of FEMA, I saw no reason to deny the request.

The various agencies with which we worked gradually began seeing the difference in temperament between Joe and me, so like children who have learned which parent is more responsive to a request for money, they began coming to me. This, in turn, helped me develop a good relationship with the White House staff because I was willing to make things happen.

Joe also hated testifying before Congress. Since I knew what was going on and was Joe's closest adviser, I became a regular on Capitol Hill. I would give testimony to the lawmakers. I would give speeches on behalf of FEMA. And soon I became the face of FEMA throughout Washington and was the "go to" guy within the agency.

The complete history of my Washington career is not important here, though I moved up to the deputy director's position with FEMA, was confirmed as its director after Joe resigned, and eventually was confirmed by the Senate as Under Secretary for Homeland Security. I fought hard for funding to plan for catastrophic disasters and encouraged the strengthening of relationships between the federal agency and its state, local, and tribal partners in anticipating, preparing for, and reacting to natural disasters. I proved how effective the agency could be when Florida governor Jeb Bush and I worked together between August and October 2004, successfully handling four consecutive hurricanes that struck the Florida coast. This was the worst series of natural disasters to strike one area in approximately a three-month period. There was minimal loss of life and minimal loss of property, which George Bush, Jeb's brother, and the *National Journal* credited for enabling him to win a second term as president. Florida was ultimately the key state in that election; if officials had mishandled the storms' aftermath or the needs of the state's residents, it is doubtful the state would have stayed Republican.

It was for all my work and the handling or assisting in numerous disasters including the attack on New York City and the Pentagon on September 11, 2001, that I was named under secretary.

My critics thought it should be a position given only to a top military official. Others thought it should go to a medical expert or someone from one of the other sciences. In the end, though, it was obvious that what was required was someone who could bring together all necessary experts relative to an impending crisis, use their expertise to develop appropriate responses, and coordinate relief. What was not obvious when I accepted the position was the need to gird up my loins to do battle against NIMBI.

Some people afflicted with NIMBI thinking lack compassion for those in sudden need due to storms, droughts, wars, and other horrors. Others seem to have an emotional disconnect between their life experiences and those of people displaced by crisis. And still others seem to feel that if they are not directly and immediately affected, the best course of action is to wait—hold meetings, create study groups, ask for reports—letting a problem simmer or explode so that the options are reduced to just one or two responses.

The position I held within the government is not one for which anyone can train. My appointment came at a time when we were living with what might be called the certainty of the uncertain. I knew some of the problems I would be confronted with each time the President declared a disaster—something that happened more than 160 times between my hiring and Hurricane Katrina. For example, when terrorists hijacked planes and used them as flying bombs to try and destroy both the World Trade Towers and portions of the Pentagon, President Bush immediately put me on the Consequence Management Committee and other groups within the White House working to respond to the attacks. He sent me along with Secretary of State Colin Powell and Governor Jeb Bush to evaluate need and coordinate American aid following the tsunami in Southeast Asia. I organized and dispatched medical teams to Bam, Iran, following the 2003 earthquake, coordinated the activities following the *Columbia* space shuttle disaster, and was responsible for all relief efforts following the four hurricanes that struck Florida in 2004. And those were just the high-profile disasters. In the years I worked for FEMA, and thus for the American people, I gained experience that ensured I could both anticipate the potential need following a disaster of any type and coordinate whatever resources were available for relief.

I also gained something else during my time working for FEMA and Homeland Security, and since then as an international consultant. It is a lesson that will be discussed in depth because no matter who is in power it is always the same: knowledge, competence, and preparedness can be trumped by politics and fear. I could have all the authority of the civilian equivalent of a military general, yet be thwarted by men and women who see life as photo opportunities, who so fear criticism that they delay making decisions until failure is guaranteed, or who are so overwhelmed by the magnitude of a challenge that they become indifferent to the suffering that only rapid action can ease. I worked in a Republican administration, but I am talking about human concern that transcends political parties. What I call deadly indifference and the failures of those whose philosophy revolves around what is in their best interest have transcended political parties, theologies, and even international alliances. This indifference and these failures have happened at least since the time of Nero. He was so hated for his self-indulgence and was so indifferent to the Romans that when a conflagration was destroying the city of Rome, it was rumored that he was hiding in his palace in Antium, giving concerts on the harplike cithara. However, it was not true that he was hiding and he rushed back to Rome to lead the firefighting efforts. But his history of indifference caused the citizens to assume the worst from their emperor, that indeed, Nero fiddled while Rome burned.

There are hundreds of examples throughout history, but two experiences in recent decades show what can happen when a nation's leaders become indifferent or disengaged. The first, the response to the certainty in the 1950s that the Soviet Union would use the atomic bomb against one or another city in the United States, involved what came to be known as Duck and Cover. The second was my experience with Hurricane Katrina. While those two examples have very disparate concerns, the similarities in the way many politicians handled these two crises show that NIMBI is too frequently the response to any situation where truth becomes uncomfortable for those who must speak it.

WHEN WE WERE YOUNG AND NAIVE

The year was 1951 and the Soviets were coming. Of that "fact" most Americans, including members of the Truman administration, were absolutely certain.

Six years earlier, on August 6, 1945, the United States had dropped an atomic bomb on the Japanese city of Hiroshima. A year after that, in 1946, author John Hersey wrote a lengthy article in the *New Yorker* magazine dramatically re-creating the horror of approximately a hundred thousand people—Japanese citizens and Korean prisoner of war laborers—being vaporized, burned, crushed, suffocated, or otherwise destroyed (often in a matter of seconds) following the blast. The magazine-length article was republished in book form and became an instant best seller that proved eerily calming for the American people.

Yes, the devastation of both Hiroshima and Nagasaki, a second city to be destroyed prior to the Japanese surrender, was horrific and caused many to question the use of the bombs. However, the explosions brought the war to an end, preventing the greater death toll predicted if an invasion of the Japanese mainland had been necessary. They also accomplished something else. They convinced many Americans, including members of the Truman administration, that there would never be another war on the same scale. Our allies would feel safe, like small boys cradled in the arms of an older, stronger, braver big brother as they went about their business, secure in the knowledge that we would again use the atomic bomb if they were threatened. And, we believed, our enemies would use negotiation and reason, not their armed forces, to find their place in a more peaceful world so we wouldn't vaporize their cities.

But always underlying everyone's thinking, planning, and attitude toward national security was the fact that only the United States had the bomb, and though it was presumed that the Soviet Union would try to find the secret, the sometimes less than competent U.S. intelligence officers did not realize how effective the Soviet spy apparatus had become. That was why Truman's advisers assured him that there would be at least a ten-year gap between Hiroshima and whenever the Soviet Union tested its first bomb. Instead, it was 1949 when the United States lost its position as the world's sole nuclear power.

* * *

First you have to know what happens when an atomic bomb explodes. You'll know when it comes, we hope it never comes, but we must be ready. . . .

If you are not ready, if you do not know what to do, then it could hurt you in different ways. It could knock you down hard, or throw you against a tree or a wall. . . . But if you duck and cover, like Bert [a turtle whose character served to educate children about atomic bomb safety], it will be much safer. You know how bad sunburn can feel, the atomic bomb flash could burn you worse than a terrible sunburn, especially where you are not covered. Now you and I do not have shells to climb into like Bert the turtle so we have to cover up in our own way.

—From the script of *Duck and Cover*,
a civil defense film shown in 1951

The truth about the atomic bomb that was known to the world's scientists and political leaders was that there was no realistic way to protect the general population from an atomic blast. Drop the bomb and people die. Those closest to the epicenter of the blast would likely be vaporized. Those farther out would die more slowly from radiation poisoning, burn trauma, and other factors, depending upon where they were located when the blast struck. There would also be those trapped in collapsed buildings, drowned when their cars dropped from shattered bridges, and otherwise killed. And no one could stop it.

During this period of recent American history, three factors impacted American society. First, World War II was over; young men returned home to marry their sweethearts and start their families without worrying that an enemy nation would challenge all they held dear. Developers bought large tracts of land at the edges of cities and constructed mass housing where the baby boomer generation would be raised. The lifestyle was perceived as being idyllic, especially since there was a sense of security that caused many families to let their children race back and forth through the neighborhood, going in and out of their friends' houses. Any "bad guys" were either relegated to the poor areas of the inner city or had been vanquished during World War II. The greatest challenge the world had ever faced was won by American GIs and their allied forces.

And then the Soviet Union exploded its atomic bomb.

* * *

First you duck, then you cover, and very lightly you cover the back of your neck and your face. Duck and cover underneath any table or desk, or anything else nearby. . . . Our civil defense workers, our men in uniform will do everything they can to warn us before enemy planes could bring a bomb near us. You may be in your schoolyard playing when the signal comes. That signal means to stop whatever you are doing and get to the nearest safe place fast.

—*Duck and Cover*

The reality of what is now often called the atomic age is that no one had any idea how to keep the civilian populace from panicking over a weapon against which there was no defense. And though we did not realize it at the time, the Soviet Union created a defense "similar" to Duck and Cover to convince young children and their parents that the danger could be overcome by preparedness.

Sergei Khrushchev, son of the man who succeeded Joseph Stalin in running the Soviet Union, explained that Soviet children were not so frightened of an attack as the Americans. Many portions of the Soviet Union had experienced weeks of terror from Nazi bombings during World War II, resulting in friends, neighbors, and family members having been killed or crippled. He explained:

> After living through the horrors of German bombings, we were not frightened by the Atomic Bomb. We flaunted our courage. During civil defense classes we were told to cover ourselves with something white, preferably a sheet, in the event of a nuclear blast, to reduce the radiation impact (I don't know how effective that would have been). A joke immediately went the rounds: "If an atomic bomb explodes, cover yourself with a sheet and crawl to the cemetery, but without hurrying. Why without hurrying? So as not to cause panic." (comments made in "From the Cold War through the Looking Glass," *American Heritage*, October 1999)

And one final word from the civil defense film concerning how to survive when in a school corridor: "You duck and cover tight against the wall. . . . Remember to keep your face and the back of your neck covered tightly. Try to fall away from windows or doors with glass in them. And if the glass breaks and flies through the air, it won't cut you."

Yes, it was almost all nonsense, and yet schools had regular Duck and Cover civil defense drills, and teachers explained how parents would drive to the school to pick them up when the all clear was sounded.

Military officials involved with the Duck and Cover program admitted that it was meant to reassure families, but not all teachers were naive or let their students believe the fantasies being woven on television, in films, or through other means.

Other suggestions proliferated, including the building of a home fallout shelter in which a family could stay for at least a few days. Never mind that the half-life of the radioactive material might be thousands of years. Everyone should remain calm. The government had it all under control.

The bomb wasn't dropped. The Russians did not invade, and eventually the Soviet Union fell apart. But other enemies arose, often hiding in mountain villages in the Middle East. Suicidal religious terrorists hijacked American airliners and crashed them into the World Trade Center Towers in New York and the Pentagon in Washington. Anthrax went through the mail, though the source has never been connected with the air assaults. And again the government was faced with a possibility for which there was no defense—biological or chemical attack or disaster. This was the new bomb and Tom Ridge, Secretary of Homeland Security, created the new, improved, twenty-first-century version of Duck and Cover. Tom told the public to stockpile duct tape and plastic sheeting. [*Note:* An Internet search of various news organizations reveals consistently that Tom Ridge made this comment. At the same time, my memory is such that I think the crediting to Ridge may have been a media myth. I remember Dave Paulison, the U.S. Fire Administrator who succeeded me, making a variation of this comment originally.] Then, when there was a warning of chemical or biological terrorism, the prepared homeowner, presumably working with his or her spouse or children, would carefully place plastic sheeting over doors and windows, sealing it with duct tape. It was cheap, seemingly efficient, and only late-night comedians dared to note it was patently ridiculous.

But did Tom Ridge's advice calm an anxious populace? Yes, perhaps because there was nothing available as an alternative. In fact, Home Depot stores around the country often tripled their sales of the tape and some managers built displays of home security essentials—bottled water, flashlights with extra batteries, duct tape, and plastic sheeting.

There was no evidence of panic to concern George W. Bush in the same manner it had Harry Truman and Dwight Eisenhower. There was also no meaningful planning or defense. In the event of a chemical or biological attack, duct tape and plastic sheeting would have saved no lives—but finding the corpses of the victims would be much easier, assuming the house had not been also obliterated by a nuclear blast.

* * *

I would learn one other lesson at the end of my tenure with the Bush White House. Leaders, unless far more courageous than most of the men and women who have risen to the top of a government bureaucracy, want what might be called a scapegoat exit strategy. This requires a person, usually with an important title, who makes a large salary and has access to every aspect of each crisis he or she is handling.

For example, as will be discussed later in this book, I earned the respect of senior White House officials for my handling of the horrendous 2004 fire season on the West Coast. It was a time of physical devastation reminiscent of the devastation of the European countryside deliberately firebombed during World War II. The story was frightening, especially in areas such as Los Angeles and San Diego where many rich and famous live in scenic splendor. Camera crews from news organizations from throughout the world were there, and I was the face and coordinator of government response in my position as director of FEMA. The higher-ups praised me for my work, and then took their own bows for having had the insight and the foresight to hire a man (me) who, though a lawyer, was so capable that he could coordinate disasters worse than others had ever seen.

What would have happened had everything gone wrong because no one listened to my requests for equipment, personnel, and other necessities? What would have happened if I had made promises my position with FEMA meant I should have been able to make, promises that, when heeded, would have ended the disaster, but were undercut by higher-ups? I would have been publicly berated and fired by the same people who made the final—wrong—decisions.

Giving me credit made the leaders look good and gave them a boost when seeking reelection. Keeping me where no one would know that those same leaders had ignored valid needs and workable plans was the scapegoat exit strategy. Everyone stayed one step removed. Everyone focused on image. Credit was lavishly given when the right actions were allowed. Blame was falsely assigned when the wrong actions were demanded despite appropriate information and requests having been provided in a timely manner.

Such lessons would be hard to accept, but I have also come to recognize that this is a potential problem with all people in power, no matter how comfortable I might be or have been with their politics.

All of which brings me to the lessons of Hurricane Katrina. Let us look in detail at this classic example of what happens when politicians' actions exhibit deadly indifference to the realities of the unavoidable.

CHAPTER 2

A LITTLE BACKGROUND

IN AUGUST 2005 I became the third most powerful person in the country confronting the impending disaster of Hurricane Katrina, a storm that would take hundreds of lives and destroy most of one of the great cities in the nation.

Katrina was not unexpected. The storm had been building in intensity, gradually approaching the Florida Keys and the Gulf of Mexico with all the force of a military assault. Dozens of federal and state agencies were on high alert and ready to supply whatever relief would be needed as the storm passed through each of their regions, having started their monitoring and planning while the soon-to-be-hurricane was still a tropical storm in the Atlantic. The movement of rescue workers and supplies—food, water, shelter, medical care, financial assistance—would be swift and adaptable because hurricanes have minds of their own. They are like bulls in a rodeo ring, seemingly aiming in one direction then shifting here and there as though on an impulsive, self-directed sightseeing tour. This was the problem, though I did not realize it at the time: exactly how that uncertainty was affecting politicians' decisions in the regions where the hurricane might strike.

The random nature of hurricanes was something I understood. In the past we might see a hurricane traveling with such force that it was certain to flatten a Florida coastal community, for example, only to have it veer off by a hundred miles. The city that had been expected to bear the brunt of the storm had homes boarded and the occupants evacuated. The community caught by surprise had inadequately prepared residents. The community we thought would need disaster relief had only disgruntled citizens complaining that they were forced to evacuate for nothing. The community caught in the unexpected hurricane shift had residents who lost pets, possessions, or family members. The survivors were angry, certain they had been betrayed by the "experts," unable to grasp the vagaries of a storm's movement, and often wreaking political vengeance by voting out their local government leaders. Such problems could not be avoided. However, the aftermath served as a warning to politicians—mayors, city managers, and governors—facing similar decisions with future storms. React before you know what you are reacting against and constituents will be outraged if you're wrong. React when you are certain of what you are acting against and you may be too late. This was certainly the problem with Louisiana and its most famous city, New Orleans.

I had been coordinating the anticipated response and recovery efforts for the aftermath of Hurricane Katrina well before the storm reached full strength. Not that the public realized at the time how much study and planning had gone into preparation and to what degree the President had been briefed. Instead, in the days and weeks following Katrina's landfall, the most familiar initials in big government came into play—CYA (cover your ass).

Hurricane Katrina was our major concern at the end of August and early part of September 2005. On August 29, 2005, nineteen hours before Hurricane Katrina slammed into the shore along the Louisiana coast, I was briefing President Bush, Homeland Security Chief (my boss) Michael Chertoff, and local officials on the readiness plans. Max Mayfield, the director of the National Hurricane Center, explained the severity of the hurricane and the fact that the storm covered a much wider area than had been seen in the past. He was certain that there was a good chance the levees would be breached, an action that would flood New Orleans. Anyone with any experience in natural disasters knows those classic disasters we all discuss and anticipate. New Orleans was one of those. Below sea level, we always knew New Orleans could turn into a fishbowl if the levees failed. Now, here was my good friend and fellow Oklahoman, Max Mayfield, director of the National Hurricane Center, telling the governor of Louisiana and the mayor of New Orleans that the theory could easily turn into the reality.

I explained that Mayor Ray Nagin and his staff had settled on their Superdome stadium as the place of last refuge. I said that the choice was highly questionable. The Superdome was twelve feet below water level, protected only if the levees held, and the roof did not seem structurally sound enough to withstand the storm. In addition, because there had been no evacuation, conditions were likely to overwhelm available state and local rescue personnel. I explained that I was certain this was likely to be the big national disaster for which we had trained, and I was concerned that there were not enough supplies and personnel in position to safely ride out the storm, then immediately move in to effect search and rescue.

President Bush said nothing during the closed-circuit videoconference. He had no questions, expressed no concerns. However, after the storm hit, when there was criticism of problems that should have been avoided, he immediately went into CYA mode. Four days following his participation in the video conference while at his ranch in Crawford, Texas, he told the Associated Press, "There is frustration but I want people to know that help's coming. I don't think that anybody anticipated the breach of the levees."

The President came through, rightly so, as a man who cared, who was concerned that the government do everything possible after being surprised by the intensity of the storm. In truth, it seemed to me that either he did not pay any attention to Mayfield's warning or he lied. These two possibilities became known only when the Associated Press obtained a copy of the videoconference and aired it nationally—six months after the fact. By then I was no longer part of the government.

Had I not been a scapegoat, someone else would have been. The reality of government, any government, is that when leadership morphs into deadly indifference, as you will witness in the chapters that follow, there are those who will do anything to keep their jobs. They fear that often what is best for the people they were elected or appointed to serve may not be in their own best interest, and NIMBI becomes the de facto consideration for both planning and response.

CHAPTER 3

THEY WARNED ME THERE'D BE STORMS LIKE KATRINA

AS THE STORM named Katrina drew closer to the United States, the more certain we were that it would strike New Orleans, perhaps the most vulnerable large city in the nation. Most Americans know of New Orleans for its unique culture, its food, and its music. They do not know that New Orleans is so far below sea level that without the manmade levees or dikes, the water would reclaim it, destroying almost everything in its path.

Hurricanes are familiar experiences along the Gulf Coast and the levees had been built to withstand *most* storms. The stronger the levee, the more it cost to build and maintain. As with so many projects that precede a need instead of being initiated in response, the levees were constructed to withstand the intensity of storms that typically strike the Gulf Coast.

There are five categories of hurricanes that strike somewhere in the world each year. These range from Category 1, with wind speeds of from 75 to 94 miles per hour, to Category 5, with wind speeds over 156 miles per hour. We talk about a hurricane as being "major" when it reaches a Category 3, with winds between 111 and 130 miles per hour, or faster. This is a storm that is fairly common but one you cannot safely ride out in your home. It is also the harshest type of storm likely to strike the Gulf Coast. Since the levees were built at a time when Louisiana, Mississippi, and other states in the region had not experienced a hurricane more severe than Category 3, it was decided to build the levees strong enough to withstand wind and driving rain at that level. Yes, Category 4 and 5 storms would still occur, but so infrequently that someone born and raised in New Orleans might not experience one in his or her lifetime. Thus, asking for the funds needed to build levees to protect the populace from such storms created a "NIMBI moment" for the politicians. Spending money on stronger levees would be seen as a wise investment only if they were needed. So long as they were not needed, the politicians looked like good stewards of taxpayer money for not seeking additional funding.

In August 2005, Katrina seemed to show why the lower-priced levees had made sense. The hurricane reached both Categories 4 and 5 in strength while in the Gulf, but as in the past, it was a sustained Category 3 when it struck the levees. What no one considered was the one additional expense that had been ignored—proper maintenance of the levees to ensure they retained their original strength.

Those of us in charge of the response effort in the cities affected by Hurricane Katrina were relieved when the winds dropped to Category 3. It was so common in Florida that Governor Jeb Bush needed little federal help when some of that state's coastal cities were battered. The public knew how to protect their homes, the evacuation routes that could be taken without panic or the risk of gridlock, and where they could stay until the storm passed over. In fact, in addition to working with the Florida governor concerning his needs, I was able to utilize some of his state's resources to help other regions of the country. We all should have been relieved by the diminishing strength of the storm as it touched land. Instead, the levees failed to hold back the water because, as would be determined in a class action lawsuit settled almost four years later, the Army Corps of Engineers and the local levee districts had failed to maintain the levees. Erosion and other problems, all expected according to reports going back at least forty years, so weakened the structure that the Category 3 protection failed. Disaster on a scale at once both horrendous and avoidable took place and no one in New Orleans was safe.

I had been working with experts from myriad agencies to plot the course of Katrina as it increased in intensity over the Florida Keys and into the Gulf of Mexico. We had been anticipating the critical supplies needed for evacuation and survival at each potential landing site. Katrina, like all other hurricanes, was meandering here and there, though always heading in the direction of New Orleans. We did not know about the failure of the Army Corps of Engineers, to be discussed later in this book. What we knew was that even with a Category 3 hurricane, the vagaries of such storms meant that the city of New Orleans would have to be evacuated. At least there was no question in my mind.

FEMA had no authority to order anyone to do anything. All we could do was suggest that ordering a mandatory evacuation was the most prudent way to save lives. It was still several days before the storm would strike with all its force, and both the state of Louisiana and the city of New Orleans had developed disaster evacuation plans months earlier. We thought that once we shared our concerns and explained our recommended actions, the mayors and governors of the affected regions would act immediately.

Louisiana governor Kathleen Blanco was almost halfway through her term and inexperienced in handling a regional disaster. She astutely recognized that there was one man whose cooperation was critical despite their political rivalry, New Orleans mayor Ray Nagin, the man who would be in the center of whatever took place. I was third, an outsider, and someone who would never have to face an election if my actions were wrong.

Earlier I mentioned that some people in critical positions delay taking action for fear of being wrong. In this case it was undeniably true that, as with any hurricane, even the best predictions could be wrong and the storm could shift direction and never strike the Louisiana coast.

I react to this kind of thinking with cynicism. I don't care what hardships people face when evacuating their neighborhoods. Their lives matter more to me than their being inconvenienced, losing a few days' pay, or having to take their children out of school. And if I could give an evacuation order, I would tell people to leave right away, while they can still get somewhere safe. I want to have all the supplies they will need in place so there will be food, medical care, and a place to sleep.

For Mayor Nagin, the issue was a variant of what I was looking at. What if the storm veers at the last minute? People's lives will have been radically inconvenienced, needless expenses incurred by the city's safety forces, and numerous other concerns will have to be addressed.

And I thought, "so what?" Here is a storm that may destroy a city. It can't be stopped. It can't be shot from the sky. Whatever is going to happen will, in large measure, be determined by how well the levees had been constructed and maintained. If their maintenance was inadequate, it is too late to fix anything.

But what if it veered in a different direction?

Both the mayor and the governor were briefed constantly on what was happening with the storm. They all understood that mandatory evacuations required a minimum of seventy-two hours to accomplish. They also understood that voluntary evacuations could mean death and devastation.

But what if the storm veered? And what if when it veered, residents of New Orleans who had been inconvenienced or hurt financially decided to sue the city? I wasn't concerned because it did not matter. Saving lives was the priority. Unfortunately New Orleans Mayor Nagin had a different priority and felt he had to consider the consequences if New Orleans was held responsible for what might be millions of dollars in damages.

As the storm was bearing down, indecision was fueled by fear. Mayor Nagin sat down with his city attorney to make certain he could not be sued. By the time he assured himself he could respond to an unavoidable disaster without being hauled into court, and by the time he issued the request to the governor and the governor gave me the request I needed to initiate the response that had been planned for *weeks*, the storm struck with such force that rescue workers from throughout the country had to wait for the violence to subside. Otherwise we would have had to rescue or recover the original rescue workers. In fact, the teams we had placed in the Superdome in response to Mayor Nagin designating it a "shelter of last resort" were asked to leave by the Louisiana National Guard once they realized how severe the storm was.

Looking back at Katrina's damage to New Orleans I realize that what I encountered was the perfect *political* storm. There was driving wind reaching well over 100 miles per hour. There was pouring rain blown by the wind; it went from a downfall to a wall of water surging against houses and high-rises. And there was the most coveted award awaiting those local politicians who had the tenacity to seek high ground before the storm hit, then fight the immediate aftermath with the ultimate weapons at their disposal—spontaneous press conferences, photo opportunities, and what could have been the wisdom of hindsight if they had started with any awareness at all.

* * *

By now you may be thinking to yourself that this is going to be a bitter memoir or a condemnation of one political party or another. You may even remember the ultimate kiss of death for any high-level presidential appointee, the President's praise in the midst of disaster, and think this is a partisan chapter. You're wrong. The problems FEMA and the Department of Homeland Security encountered will occur again and again; natural disasters are no respecter of political parties, politicians' egos, or anything else, and those same politicians will fail to deal with uncomfortable realities they cannot prevent.

CHAPTER 4

THE CITY BUILT UNDER WATER

One might argue that New Orleans is equal parts Creole cooking, zydeco music, and hubris. What other city in the United States so proudly courts impending disaster with each excessive rainfall, each tropical storm, and each approaching freighter?

The residents of the area most prone to natural disaster damage often developed a bravado toward their living conditions and indifference to the fact that each storm was unique. Katrina would be just one in a long line of survival threats they or their families had endured, and some anticipated the hurricane in the tradition of people who had known the futility of fighting fate and the joy of seizing the moment for pleasure—they partied. In some sections, as the skies slowly blackened, the winds increased, and everyone knew that power failures were coming, people brought out the barbecue grills. They cooked and shared their food because everyone knew that it would likely spoil otherwise. They danced and played music with the certainty that once again they would be spared the ravages that such hurricanes can bring.

The nightclubs remained open for their own partying; owners chose not to cancel the entertainers booked for the weekend and took only minimal precautions to protect the buildings from the storm. Katrina was not the first assault by Mother Nature, nor would it be the last. And unless the mayor, the governor, and other officials said this one was different, the inescapable big one, it would be just another scary storm story to tell their grandchildren.

The unique danger to New Orleans, and one too often overlooked by long-term residents, is that this is not a city with a beachfront stretching below houses, apartments, and businesses in the manner of San Diego or Miami. Instead it is a beachfront with a city stretching below, the bottom of a bowl that is six feet lower than the water's edge. Lake Pontchartrain, the Mississippi River, and the nearby Gulf of Mexico are all lapping at its perimeter, constantly trying to get in.

Not that New Orleans is helpless. Most of us have heard of the famous levees and many who slept through geography in school tend to think of them as natural protection on which people work, play, and enjoy the view. In truth they were built by the Army Corps of Engineers starting in the late 1800s. Eventually the main defense against unstoppable flooding involved an earthen levee (think Holland's dikes and the little Dutch boy). This soil had to be rigid, stable, and strong to withstand the forces of the water currents constantly moving against it in normal times and smashing like thirty-foot-high bulldozers during annual hurricanes. To this was added sheet piling (a thin metal wall) and poured concrete.

Each levee, when seen up close, looks like an impenetrable fortress wall capable of withstanding the endless assault of natural and predictable harsh weather conditions. From afar you see a thin gray line of concrete that has to be maintained and reinforced before even the smallest leak appears. There is no drainage from the city. If water pours in through a break in the levee, it pools in the lowest parts of the city. It will not flow back out. To compensate for this problem, New Orleans uses pumps to push the water to the outside of the levees for drainage.

The nightmare aftermath of Hurricane Katrina started at the confluence of political wrangling and fiscal irresponsibility. The U.S. Army Corps of Engineers had known for years that the foundation for the levees was substandard and not safe to build on. One of the major negative reports to the Corps' Board of Contract Appeals had been made by Pittman Construction back in 1998. There were also maintenance concerns dating back at least forty years.

What was about to happen during Hurricane Katrina was both easy to anticipate and impossible to predict. First there was the quality of the protection for which the levees had been designed. Most hurricanes that touch cities in the United States were historically no more powerful than a Category 3. This meant that the government had a choice. They could have Louisiana levees built to withstand Category 3 hurricanes, knowing that there was a good chance they would never have to protect the city from anything more powerful, or they could assume the worst, that there would come a day when a Category 4 or 5 storm struck New Orleans. Choosing the latter was much more expensive. Taxpayers might be irate that so much money was spent on something that seemed useless year after year. Voters might decide that the mayor and the governor were misspending taxpayer money and vote them out of office. It was better to build for the predictable need and hope it would be many years, if ever, before greater protection was required.

This decision-making process had its corollary when a hurricane was bearing down on the city at a speed that was greater than the levees could handle. Politicians were desperate for two outcomes. The first was to not look as though they made a mistake, and the second was to look heroic in the aftermath, regardless of what they did or did not do to help. All together it creates the perfect political storm.

* * *

On July 23, 2004, those of us involved with homeland security, a term that included natural disasters, deadly accidents, disease pandemics, terrorism, and other extraordinary acts, went before Congress and the Bush administration to request money for catastrophic planning. I had decided shortly after being asked to chair a homeland security transition team creating the new Department of Homeland Security that I would make catastrophic disaster planning one of my priorities and, hopefully, a legacy of my tenure, however long.

The problem we were facing was explained most effectively by Robert Block, a staff reporter for the *Wall Street Journal,* in an article that appeared on August 16, 2004. He wrote:

> Emergency managers who feel Homeland Security's approach to disasters underweights the natural variety point to the ODP, which has a traditional law-enforcement focus and is heavily staffed with former police officers. "The problem is that federal

law enforcement has very limited experience with natural disasters but now has the greatest influence on the way the new programs are being structured," says Frances Edwards, director of the Office of Emergency Services in San Jose, Calif. Emergency managers sometimes refer to the ODP as "the gun-toters."

Homeland Security officials maintain that equipment and training to respond to a terrorist attack is also good preparation for dealing with natural disasters. Ms. Edwards and many other emergency-management officials dispute that reasoning. "A terrorist attack, even a bad one like 9/11, is a single-site event," Ms. Edwards says. "You can't say that about earthquakes, where buildings can collapse all over the place. Preparing for terrorism doesn't prepare you for everything—but the opposite is true: If you are prepared for catastrophic natural disasters, you are prepared for any catastrophic terrorist event."

While funds and gear to fight terrorism are readily available, funds to help states mitigate disasters have been cut in half since 2001. For instance, after flooding in northeast Iowa in May damaged or destroyed more than 200 homes and businesses, the state found that funds for post-disaster mitigation were insufficient for their needs, under formulas set by Congress and agreed to by the Homeland Security Department. ("Hurricane Tests Emergency Agency at Time of Ferment")

Funding requests like this are always tricky. We had no immediate danger to point to when making our request. We also knew that there were those politicians who felt that by naming a potential problem you had somehow caused it. However, we recognized that it was precisely because there was no immediate threat that we needed to do the work.

People often assume that cities, states, and counties are prepared for catastrophic events. Law enforcement agencies have evacuation plans; though they are often planned in great detail they are quite limited. This is because they are created for sporting events and other forms of entertainment that draw large regional crowds. The evacuation plans are designed to quickly and safely move what may be thousands of cars from the stadium, arena, or other site to the residential sections of the city and suburbs. Not only is the end—the drivers' homes—known when police direct the traffic, the only people involved are the ones whose presence adds no additional burdens to the community.

The evacuation necessary for a disaster is quite different. If you go from an entertainment venue to your home you will have everything you need for survival—food, water, shelter, and so on in your home, and familiar supermarkets and restaurants all along your journey. Local businesses know what to stock for their customer base and everything is stable. However, with a disaster the police and other first responders are not directing you to your home. The stores that have supplies may be closed or in ruins. Your personal concern becomes getting to the nearest community that has the resources you need— hotels and other shelters, food, transportation. But once you arrive in that community, all the resources have been planned around the existing, stable population. The evacuation may double or triple the number of people demanding the same limited resources. Food shortages quickly arise. Hotels are instantly overcrowded. Fuel supplies may run low. And if the disaster is widespread enough, the people evacuating from the disaster area will pass right through on to a second community, their ranks enlarged by residents of the city initially designated as the evacuation site. The farther from the site of the disaster people must travel, the more people there are traveling and the faster all resources are overwhelmed.

Each carefully planned evacuation is its own disaster waiting to happen. Planning must take into account all contingencies, because there is never a single problem. Most disaster plans within a community are shortsighted—How do we safeguard our residents, including moving them to a different location? What happens after that is rarely considered in a meaningful way. Worse, with some disasters, from hurricanes and tornadoes to a hazardous chemical waste spill, it may be necessary to establish facilities that can hold large numbers of people for days or weeks in a location unprepared to receive them.

Congress understood the need for the planning we proposed and we were provided with the funds to look at the most likely scenarios that could affect the nation. Some were natural events that happened on a regular basis—hurricanes, tornadoes, earthquakes. Some were occasional events such as an influenza pandemic. Some resulted from enemy action, whether from an American extremist or an attack by people from outside the United States.

Because of the limitations of time and money, we narrowed the list to the five most likely disasters the nation could face. Certainly the one the public most feared was an attack by enemy governments, a concern the nation had been dealing with since the Cold War. Before the fall of the Soviet Union it was discovered that Bulgarians working for the Russian KGB had been studying Manhattan Island, the most densely populated borough of New York City. They noticed that high-rise apartments had been built like rows of dominoes. Set the right type and amount of explosives at the base of one apartment and it would fall toward the next. Do the same to each apartment in line and thousands could die as their apartments collapsed, each building falling into the next.

The public also feared enemy assaults on critical infrastructure, from destroying freeways on the West Coast to poisoning water supplies.

All these fears were valid but we wanted to start with the most likely problem facing the nation—a recurring natural disaster. For each human-engineered incident—a bomb, sabotage, the deliberate release of deadly chemicals—there are probably a dozen or more natural disasters. These include floods, droughts, tornadoes, hurricanes, and forest fires, each of which can be far more destructive than anything caused by a terrorist. That is why, when we ranked the five disasters most likely to occur in the near future, we realized that number one on our list had to be a hurricane hitting New Orleans.

The other four on our list also ranked higher than any danger from an outside enemy. These included a hurricane along the East Coast that would strike Manhattan or Boston, the New Madrid Fault causing a massive earthquake in the American Midwest, the San Andreas Fault creating a massive earthquake on the West Coast, and a tsunami hitting the Oregon/Washington coast. Also important for our planning was the fact that all choices were events that were known to have occurred, albeit often in the distant past, and were likely to occur again.

Our selection was based on many factors, including weather patterns and geological studies. Some events, such as a tsunami in the Northwest, are cyclical over hundreds or thousands of years. A tsunami could start from movement under the Pacific Ocean and endanger the Washington/Oregon coastline. By contrast, an earthquake such as have occurred along the San Andreas Fault is always inland. As to their predictability, all we knew for certain was that such disasters had happened and would happen again. They might not occur tomorrow. They might not happen in anyone's lifetime or even the next century. That was why we made them lower priorities on our list. Hurricanes, annual events that strike parts of the U.S. coastline with varying force, became our highest priority. And among the cities that realistically might be struck in any year, the most vulnerable to catastrophic destruction was New Orleans.

Many have asked about the future of a city as fragile as New Orleans. The levees made lowland survival possible. But the protection provided by the levees, their critical maintenance needs, the maximum forces they can withstand, and the wisdom of living below water level are all best understood when everything fails. Under the best of circumstances, a major hurricane striking New Orleans would be a disaster, if only from loss of property. The potential for loss of life compounded our concerns.

We realized as we started our planning that New Orleans was in many ways almost identical to the Tampa-St. Petersburg region of Florida, where hurricanes also strike regularly. The difference is that when a hurricane strikes Tampa-St. Petersburg, the surge waters come in, flood the area, and then flow back out into the Gulf of Mexico. As I noted earlier, New Orleans is more like a fishbowl. Surge waters come in, collect in the low-lying areas, and stay there, as more and more water accumulates.

The threat assessment required us to look first at the levees, the key to protecting New Orleans. Maintain the levees and they could be counted upon to hold back the water that would otherwise drown the city. If the levees were damaged before the storm hit, or if they were not strong enough to withstand the force of the storm, water would pour into New Orleans and destroy homes, businesses, and lives.

The water pressing against the levees was a concern in the best of times. During normal weather, whether periods of dry spells or times of natural rainfall, there is always a degree of seepage from underground water and sometimes normal rain. This seepage is countered around the clock through the use of pumps that continuously operate to bring the lakes back to a manageable level. Add a Category 3 or stronger hurricane into the local ecology and you always have a disaster waiting to happen.

The Indians understood the problems when they first settled New Orleans. They lived on high ground, on that portion of the land that showed no sign of ever having been flooded, raising crops and livestock despite weather conditions similar to those we encounter today.

Perhaps it was the arrogance of the white settlers who followed. Perhaps it was their faith in their ability to build the barriers that have held back the water in the past. The levees were built over time, and as they held back floodwaters, the public began to think the area was safe. They did not consider that levees could be improperly constructed, improperly maintained, or of limited protection during a natural disaster. Instead it was as though the levees were natural barriers like mountains. People thought nothing of building homes, offices, entertainment venues, and retail establishments in flood-prone areas. The flooding had not occurred, so, somehow in the convoluted thinking of those who moved there, it would not.

More time passed. The public ignored the fact that the levees were built to withstand the force of only the most frequent hurricanes, not the ones that periodically struck the coast with much greater force. Apparently the lack of Category 4 and Category 5 hurricanes made people feel secure when the levees handled the Category 3 storms. They stopped thinking that the situation, over time, would get worse. The likelihood was limited in any given year. But the likelihood was one hundred percent over time.

Security led to a degree of denial. It seemed that many of the people involved in maintenance planning believed that keeping the levees strong was a little like considering how often to paint a house. Homeowners know when time and weather have begun to damage the paint. Some starts to peel and chip. Some discolors. The house looks old before its time, and it is obvious that the old paint needs to be stripped away and replaced with fresh coats of paint. Yet the price of the work is relatively high, and the homeowner's plans for a vacation or other expense will be affected by a cost that can be avoided until the following year. Of course the exterior deteriorates a bit, but is that really so bad when the money can be set aside and the painting delayed just a few more months?

The homeowner was wrong. Of course the house needed painting. But the desire to use the money for other purposes leads to rationalization about avoiding the work and denial concerning how much it needs.

The same was true for the levees, but that would not become widely known until after Katrina struck. Maintenance had been recommended and delayed. Money that should have been set aside for critical analysis of the system and appropriate repairs was spent on other needs. And adding to what should have been an ongoing concern, the levees were only constructed to withstand Category 3 storms. Higher winds would instantly endanger the city.

The denial of the potential problems with the levees amazed me. I could understand the appeal of New Orleans with its cultural diversity. I could understand wanting to live there, especially in the areas that were on such high ground that there was reasonable assurance of safety during a storm. But what shocked me was discovering that some residents seemed so convinced that the levees would hold against any storm that they chose homes that would always be the equivalent of Ground Zero in a hurricane.

The reality of these unrealistic choices became glaringly obvious when I flew to New Orleans immediately after Katrina passed through. I made my way to the top of one of the levees to see how much of the structure was intact and what portions had broken, as well as the degree of devastation. Only then did I get a glimpse of some residents' indifference and the reason they were certain to lose all that they owned.

Directly across from where I was standing was what was left of someone's home. It had been constructed close enough to the levee for me to be able to pick up a rock and throw it through a window if any windows had been left.

Floodwaters had reached the top floor of the house and were lapping at the highest windows. A natural gas pipeline had broken some time earlier and the gas had ignited; flames were shooting from the shattered windows.

I was transfixed. This had been a family's home, built where disaster was inevitable the moment any leakage occurred from the levee that had been built God knew how many decades earlier and never properly maintained. This had been a home purchased in denial of where it was located and the fragility of their safety.

I never learned if everyone escaped unharmed, though I pray they did. Instead I witnessed both the validity of our department's planning thirteen months earlier, and the emotional and intellectual disconnect between the theoretical, on which we trained, and the reality of human reactions we could not anticipate.

In our earlier planning we created the fictional Category 5 Hurricane Pam, which would begin as a moderate storm over the Atlantic Ocean before building speed and power as it headed for New Orleans. We brought in experts in everything from structural engineering, to meteorology, law enforcement, medicine, and every other field that would be needed in a major hurricane disaster. We also hired consultants who were trained to put on this type of exercise. They brought in experts with knowledge of past storms. They set up scale models of likely landing points such as along the coasts of Florida, Mississippi, and Louisiana. They also had computer simulations of all the variables that could occur.

In addition, they prepared for the day we gathered so that they could use what they called "injects" to challenge us. Each inject represented a sudden, predictable, yet easily overlooked change to what was happening.

The exercise, conducted early in July 2004, started with the development of a typical small storm that would build in intensity over water until the winds gradually increased to the level of a hurricane. The hurricane, which we named Pam, moved in a westward direction from where it began until it endangered our East Coast.

As our theoretical storm increased in force, the various disaster experts around the table explained how civilian safety would be handled. It all seemed straightforward until the facilitators announced one of their injects. Hurricane Pam had taken a sudden shift. The anticipated location where it would strike was no longer in great danger, the evacuation of the residents unnecessary. However, while they only had to handle intense rain and wind, a community farther along the coast, one that had not taken precautions, was suddenly facing disaster.

How would the first responders be able to handle the crisis they had not anticipated, yet was common enough with major storms that it might occur? In what ways could there be an effective evacuation? What would happen when those fleeing the unexpected brunt of the hurricane entered a city that was not prepared to receive them? Where might they seek shelter? How would they be fed? What if the power went out? Each scenario was worse than the previous and all had occurred with past storms.

PROBLEMS EVERYWHERE

The exercise involving Hurricane Pam was meant to help us with a disaster that could damage or destroy New Orleans. It did, but the injects quickly made us realize how the innovations of contemporary society created the potential for greater problems.

The levees were our greatest concern, of course, but even if they held against whatever strength storm struck the coast, the response to the storm by local residents would create challenges requiring advance planning. For example, we realized that grocery stores, gas stations, and even maintenance businesses such as auto and truck repair shops all relied on innovations in computer technology to ensure "just in time" delivery. Prior to both computer and global positioning systems (GPS) use, the maintenance and replenishment of businesses was an inexact science. Supermarkets tried to stock according to the expectation of demand, such as having more turkey for sale around Thanksgiving and more ham for sale around Christmas. Sometimes a store owner would underorder to be sure of selling out. Other times an owner would make certain he or she could take the greatest possible advantage of the probable increase in demand by stocking freezer cases and coolers in a back area, or perhaps a separate building or a storage area. Employees would restock the main shopping floor as necessary.

Computers allowed for the start of just in time ordering. Restaurants, for example, could have a payment system so that each time a customer's bill was rung up, the computer knew how much food had been used by the restaurant and how much remained. The computer was doing a partial inventory with each new customer so predicting need became so well defined that large stockrooms were unnecessary. Delivery could be arranged almost to the minute when more food or other supplies were needed.

The GPS systems installed on delivery trucks operated by the suppliers enabled the most effective routing of trucks passing around the country. Empty vehicles could be dispatched to regional suppliers for pickup and delivery, the GPS system allowing the dispatchers to always know where every truck was located and alert the drivers to changes as needed. The result was a reduction in the number of square feet of space a business required to work efficiently. It also meant that if a crisis suddenly interrupted the established delivery system, food would quickly be in short supply, gasoline might be unavailable, and emergency medical supplies could not be delivered.

A disaster could expand exponentially with the breakdown of just in time delivery. That was what we found with Hurricane Pam and what we would encounter with real-life Hurricane Katrina. Even worse, having knowledge of a problem is not the same as being able to solve it. Just in time was too well entrenched in the way we handled commerce to return to a warehouse approach just because of a natural disaster. It also meant that an elaborate and reasonably flexible relief effort would be needed just to provide basic supplies, and that would be the case regardless of the disaster if people had to leave their homes and neighborhoods.

A disaster, whether natural or manmade, disrupts the normal flow of goods and critical services. Not only are critical businesses lacking the supplies they will need to feed and otherwise meet the needs of an influx of people to a community, the suppliers are not equipped for the sudden change in product demand. Some of the evacuees will stay in the community to which they flee; others will move on to the next safe community and overwhelm their resources. Almost nothing will have been warehoused. Cities couldn't justify the stockpiling of food, water, medical supplies, and cots in areas that were believed to be safe. FEMA could make plans for fairly broad regions of the country, but a meaningful response to a disaster required waiting to see where it was headed and what the needs of the people would be. A storm can shift direction, moving miles away from where it was anticipated, perhaps creating havoc with evacuees who thought they were safe only to discover that their detour put them in more danger. Exercises like the one for the fictional Hurricane Pam were meant to help both first responders and long-term relief workers and agencies understand what they could be facing. The reality, especially with a storm, is that Mother Nature frequently converts order into chaos and does it in the blink of an eye. We would never be able to anticipate change with 100 percent accuracy, but we had to be ready to shift our actions so we were at least apace with the ongoing crisis.

* * *

Sometimes the criticism of my concerns was valid. Within much of the United States the impact of a crisis may be minimal. We live in a nation of surplus, so bringing in supplies may be delayed but not long enough to be a major problem. In addition, opportunistic businesspeople will find a way to meet whatever need exists. There is even a local example near where I lived in Colorado. Periodically Interstate 70 is shut down by a snowstorm that devastates eastern Colorado. The town of Limon is perfectly positioned to receive stranded travelers, and the Red Cross immediately opens the high school gym for everyone who needs shelter. Over the next few hours, as snowplows are clearing the area, the only predictable shortages are of diapers and tampons.

However, there are other parts of the country, and many parts of the world, where a disaster is not a temporary inconvenience and lives are interrupted for more than a few hours. Evacuation takes the people to isolated locations or to locations where ease of access can be abruptly ended. To say that a solution can be found quickly may be correct, but that possibility is determined by the type of disaster—natural, manmade, or both. And even when resources such as an airlift might be possible, the logistics can be overwhelming. Just take a look at a map of Manhattan Island and think about what would happen if the bridges and tunnels were destroyed. Then add an artificially induced medical crisis caused by the release of anthrax or an outbreak of bubonic plague and you will see the type of danger the nation needs to prepare for, if only to understand what could happen.

* * *

The nature of our planning was to focus on the community-wide issues of a disaster like Pam. The injects the trainers used for our exercise included the disaster knocking out power lines, so critical services could be provided only with equipment powered by emergency generators. The generators, in turn, would need fuel, and though the fuel could be stockpiled, it was a finite resource. We could not predict when the generators would no longer be critical for hospitals and food storage equipment. We would have to be ready to either resupply the area or ensure the evacuation of the people who required generator-run medical equipment.

Further injects included trees that had fallen across roads, halting supply trucks loaded with food, water, and medical equipment. Cell phone service was lost as the exercise experienced the added problems of damaged transmitters, weak or nonexistent signals, and people being unable to recharge their cell phone batteries. Only wired phone lines had the best chance of remaining a viable form of communication over time, but how many people still used wired lines? Maybe most and maybe almost none, which meant that the most reliable form of communication was also the least likely to be available.

Again in our model, as the days passed, emergency vehicles that sustained minor damage could not be repaired because of lack of parts. Hospitals ran short of basic supplies such as sterile gloves, cleaning supplies, and other items so commonplace that no one realized they were regularly delivered just in time.

Each inject added to the crisis in our planning. Each inject showed us that the business infrastructure of our society, the one built on just in time planning and GPS-guided delivery was a major weakness. There was no way to change the use of this cost-saving technology, and it was no problem in good times. In bad times, if the Hurricane Pam exercise was correct, people living out the aftermath of our theoretical natural disaster would face rationing, gridlock, and in some areas, panic.

As we worked through the planning exercises we found ways to handle some scenarios and recognized that others could not be addressed in a meaningful way. As we always knew, there would be a degree of havoc under the best of circumstances whether a disaster was natural or manmade. All we could do was make certain we anticipated every possible problem and outcome, and then do our best to protect the public by removing them from harm's way.

"HURRICANE PAM" STRIKES NEW ORLEANS

Those sitting around the table quickly realized that disaster response on the level we were considering was a civilian operation that had to be coordinated in the same manner as a massive military maneuver. Initially we looked at the basic responsibility of providing a safe place to live and adequate food for what would be an unknown period of time between when the storm struck and when repairs were adequate for people to return home.

Transportation was another critical element. The nature of city living is such that while many people drive, many people do not. They rely on their feet, bicycles, buses, taxis, or light-rail. Transportation had to be planned for evacuating an endangered area, including determining boarding points in enough places throughout the city that everyone would have access.

Psychologists and social workers would have to be available to handle the emotional trauma of the upheaval and loss. We would also need personnel available to help those who lost everything in the storm including critical personal papers. Previous hurricanes in other parts of the country had destroyed county courthouses, federal buildings, and other repositories of paperwork necessary to document birth dates, where folks went to school, whether they graduated, employment history, and other essential details. Some of these needs were mentioned by those who had experience with such crises; some came as injects from the facilitators. All of them showed how fast an overwhelming crisis can become even worse.

The public image of a catastrophic disaster often includes the use of the National Guard. Many citizens are unaware of the realities of states' rights versus the responsibilities of the federal government. The National Guard can be activated for military duty without the approval of the governor of the state. However, if the National Guard is not needed for its primary duty, it can be used within the state for rescue work, supplementing law enforcement, transporting critical materiel, and similar matters. Such use must be authorized by the governor, which is not a problem unless a state's guard unit(s) has been deployed for action overseas.

We faced another problem. At the time we were planning for Hurricane Pam, the National Guard in many states was being called up to fight in Iraq and Afghanistan. Some units had already deployed at the time of our exercise. Others were waiting to be called up or were in training prior to leaving. They would not be available even if civilian disaster assistance was part of their primary mission, which it was not. This had to be reflected in our modeling of how a disaster and response would unfold.

Again, it was the governor and not FEMA, Homeland Security, or even the president who had primary responsibility for calling up the guard within his or her state. And the governor would likely act only when the mayor of the affected city requested such help. Disasters, unless considered an act of terrorism or war, are usually seen as local crises. The federal government supports and encourages extensive planning when possible and develops its own contingency plans. There are supply stockpiles and pharmaceutical stockpiles, all of which will be used in an affected state—once the governor puts in the call for help. And while it is considered a given that such requests will be granted, the nature of the Constitution and Supreme Court decisions concerning the rights of the states makes the request procedure a formality that cannot be avoided.

After planning for Hurricane Pam we were 100 percent sure what would happen the next time a major hurricane struck the Gulf Coast area, regardless of its strength. What we could not anticipate with any certainty was just where it would strike. That meant that we would almost certainly have to recommend the evacuation of any city that was in the path of a full force hurricane a few days before the storm's landfall. It was the only way to save lives and avoid panic, and when it was over mayors and governors would be seen as heroes for providing the warning and escape routes. By contrast, if an area was evacuated just before the storm veered off in a different direction, perhaps forcing a second evacuation, those who saw themselves as needlessly evacuated might have incurred the expense of food, hotels, lost pay, and lost production.

Admittedly planners had a rather cavalier attitude toward the evacuations we felt would be necessary for a city facing a real storm, not the theoretical Hurricane Pam. We would make the recommendation if and when the time came. We expected that our explanation of the impending crisis would be so thorough and so respected that those in charge of the evacuation—the mayors and/or governors of the affected states—would act prudently and in the best interest of the residents. We did not consider the political ramifications within a community affected by an impending disaster. After a disaster has occurred, just showing up and looking like a compassionate leader can protect a politician from immediate criticism and perhaps ensure reelection. Prior to a disaster, whatever that local politician is seen doing to prepare can lead to ridicule or praise, being retained in office or voted into oblivion.

Real life meant that *if* the storm hit as anticipated, the city's mayor would be a hero and FEMA would be coordinating the care, feeding, and ultimate recovery of the people who had been evacuated. *If* the storm veered off as had happened in the past, those evacuated would have their lives disrupted. The communities that "welcomed" the evacuees would have their infrastructure overstressed. The mayor whose order triggered all this would see his or her city struggle financially from the cost of the needless evacuation, or possibly face a lawsuit from area businesses and citizens alike. He or she would also likely lose in the next election.

The "right" decision in our eyes, the experts and administrators sitting around the table "playing" at hurricane response strategies in much the manner of Department of Defense war gamers, could be responsible for ending the careers of one or more politicians who listened to our recommendations.

THE FLAWS WE NEVER SAW

Another problem with planning exercises is that they are handled by experts looking at the most predictable problems and solutions. They bring their own thoughts and experiences, which are excellent but narrow their thinking.

Our discussion about Hurricane Pam was on human life. We wanted to safely remove those people endangered by the storm in order to save the most lives possible. Triage was the operative concept. If someone living and working at Point A would likely drown or be trapped during the disaster, we wanted to move that person to Point B where we could provide food, shelter, medical care, and whatever else was needed. Then, starting in Point B, we would move the people either back to the homes they left, assuming they were still standing and safe, or we would move them to a central location, further guaranteeing their safety while they began to figure out how to rebuild their lives.

The planning was all very logical, very humane, and a portion of it was very stupid. We wanted to save lives, but we were not looking at the lives the people we were trying to help were leading.

The first of the two most serious mistakes we made was not considering pets. I won't go so far as to talk about pets as being just like members of the family and some of the other clichés people use. What matters is that pets serve an important purpose in the lives of many people. Individuals suffering from some forms of depression, the elderly, the chronically ill, the lonely, and others with problems and circumstances that can cause them to withdraw will often use the care of a cat, dog, or other pet to stay healthier. A pet is a friend, a companion, a stabilizing influence that improves the quality of life.

I have dogs, and when traveling without them I begin to miss them. It is not the same as missing my wife or children, but animals matter and neither I nor the others involved with the planning included pets in our thinking.

We learned how foolish we had been when rescue workers encountered men and women sitting on the roofs of their homes, holding a pet and refusing to get into one of the urban search and rescue (USAR) boats without the animal. They were not about to leave their pet behind, and in some cases it was clear they were willing to stay in danger to keep the animal as safe as possible.

Rescue workers often felt they had to take people only, whether in the boats or on the buses and other vehicles used for evacuation. Animals were pulled from the hands of children. More than 15,500 pets would ultimately be saved in the two weeks following Hurricane Katrina, though others were lost and many of those whose pets might have been rescued had no way to learn where their animals might be. None of this was discussed during the Hurricane Pam exercise, though we did learn. Current disaster planning includes plans for pets, and I was pleased that a number of groups volunteered to rescue animals, provide shelter, and reunite people separated from their pets. But our work would have gone easier and with far less deserved criticism had we considered the pets from the start.

The other issue was harder to understand until you look at the way some people live. Upper-income suburbanites have a tendency to live their lives among several different areas in which they travel. Their homes are usually clustered with other houses of similar size and cost. Their employers are often clustered in an industrial park or in high-rise office buildings in a downtown location. If they are in retail sales, they may work in a shopping mall. Entertainment centers are likely to be in yet another location. And there are houses of worship, clubs, and government buildings, each likely to require more travel.

What this means is that in the course of the average day, people travel among several locations. They are familiar with large sections of their cities. They are comfortable going to new locations because they have seen a variety of areas during their typical week.

Lower-income or elderly residents of inner cities live quite different lives. Many do not own cars. Many adapt to their neighborhoods and develop a rhythm to their days that leaves them unfamiliar with more than a few blocks in each direction from their homes. They might live in an apartment over a food store or near a supermarket. Upscale suburbanites may fancy saving money by driving to different locations for their necessities. The lower-income inner-city resident recognizes the need for convenience, buying food from smaller stores where prices are higher but whose location makes them more practical. Often there is a small clothing store or a dollar-type store offering necessities such as basic work clothes, T-shirts, and the like. Chain drugstores offer more shopping options, and many are open twenty-four hours a day to serve residents who may work shifts other than the classic 9 to 5. There are restaurants, bars, and churches. Medical and dental care centers will be available, again within either walking distance or a short bus ride away. Finally there are the schools, all of which are likely to be within a mile or two of where the people are living.

This means that some people will be born in an inner-city neighborhood, go to school and a house of worship within walking distance of their home, marry someone from the area, or a similar one, and raise their children there. They are comfortable in their neighborhoods, feeling safe and secure in an area they know, albeit limited by their mobility.

An evacuation is far more frightening for someone whose life has been limited to an area such as the Lower Ninth Ward of New Orleans than it is for someone who is more familiar with the surrounding area. Everything is unknown. There is nothing with which to compare the past and the near future. These people have probably not traveled to adjoining states. And suddenly they are being uprooted; people of little means are being told to go where they have nothing.

The psychological trauma was enormous, and most people were unwilling to leave all that they had known. The governor and mayor needed people to go house to house, explaining not only the danger but where they would be going and what help would be available. After Hurricane Katrina had passed New Orleans, I found that we needed to have bus collection points fairly close together throughout the low-income areas to be evacuated so that people would not have to walk into unfamiliar areas.

These overlooked concerns were the result of our failures to consider the lives the people led and the influences on their choices. We had the broad view of upper-income individuals working for various federal agencies and comfortable with the idea of sudden travel to different parts of the country. We had not looked at the social and emotional concerns of the people who were endangered, only their physical safety. We did not realize that just leaving their immediate neighborhood or the city where they had lived all their lives created a greater fear than the danger from the storm and the possible destruction of the levees.

We made this second discovery after Katrina passed and we were trying to provide water, food, and other emergency resources to people who were still in their homes. We needed to assess their health to see who needed immediate assistance, who needed rapid evacuation, and who might be in the least danger. Going door to door would only enable us to see the condition of the person who answered. It would not tell us about people afraid to answer the door and about other people who might be inside.

We also learned that we needed to leave supplies just far enough from each home that anyone inside had to come out to get them. Professionals handling the distribution would then be better able to determine the physical condition of more people than might otherwise be checked.

* * *

Planning for a disaster was not unique to our agencies. We had more resources for what we did than any individual community. We also had broader responsibility than local first responders. However, we also knew that the cities likely to be affected during hurricane season would have done their own preplanning. They would have identified resources available for everything from identifying safe shelter areas to the location of trucks, buses, and other vehicles for moving supplies, assisting with any evacuation, and transporting the sick and injured to or from area medical centers.

Cities and the states also had mutual assistance agreements with each other so that resources around the country could be shared. The more fortunate communities would supply law enforcement, firefighters, ambulances, emergency crews to fix downed power lines, and whatever else they could spare. All resources and personnel available through the mutual assistance agreements would have been identified, both within the impacted area and the regions that surrounded it. Then, when the disaster struck, there would be an immediate analysis of the damage and the need. As the need in one community exceeded local resources, a call would be made to a state that had agreed to provide mutual assistance. Then their personnel would start streaming into the damaged region. Both the mayor and the governor of the affected region would reach out to those with whom the assistance agreement had been made. They would operate independently of one another since usually their needs and available resources were different, but always within a unified command structure.

If the governor determined that all available resources under his or her control were inadequate or soon to be exhausted, the governor would turn to FEMA, which would be ready to find and coordinate whatever was needed, including helicopters, trucks, boats, and cars, none of which FEMA owns or maintains. But FEMA does have the power of monetary resources and applicable laws to reach out to other states and other federal departments and agencies to deploy those kinds of resources. While many of the medical teams, rescue teams, and other personnel are provided training and resources by FEMA, these individuals and teams are generally not FEMA employees but employees of local fire departments, rescue squads, and paramedic units. Despite what many critics claim, FEMA does not possess the resources and personnel to respond on the ground in a disaster; it only has teams to coordinate the deployment of state, local, and federal personnel.

NEITHER FEMA NOR HOMELAND SECURITY HAVE AN ARMY

Some people believe that either FEMA or the Department of Homeland Security has an army of people ready to enter a disaster area by land, sea, or air. They think the system operates like the climactic scene of one of those World War II movies during which thousands of men parachute from hundreds of planes. Each man is equipped to fight the moment he lands on the ground and the sheer number of combat-experienced veterans overwhelms the enemy and saves the day. Instead, we had fewer full-time personnel serving the nation than comprise many major city police forces.

Disaster response involves two critical resources. The first resource involves several strategically placed supply centers. The federal government has several regionally placed warehouses holding everything from emergency generators to cots, meals ready to eat (MREs), drinking water, laptop computers, radios, lighting equipment, blankets, medical supplies, and everything else large numbers of people might need when relocated. Other facilities, usually specially renovated space in poultry processing plants, are carefully maintained temperature- and climate-controlled storage areas for the most likely pharmaceuticals to be needed in an emergency.

The poultry plant facilities sound odd or like something meant to be hidden from enemy attack. In truth, such plants, rented in conjunction with the Department of Health and Human Services (HHS), provide the least expensive storage and are located near areas providing access to rail, truck, and air routes. The conditions needed to keep meat safe are the same as those needed to keep pharmaceuticals fresh. However, the two are never commingled. The pharmaceuticals are protected in a massive area within the larger plant, a little like the safe deposit box area within a bank or savings and loan.

The rented space, like the meat storage area, has elaborate backup systems in case of power failure. These ensure that whenever medications are taken from storage to the disaster site they will provide their intended health benefits.

Another factor in our Hurricane Pam planning was determining how we would move the stockpiled supplies to the areas where they were needed. The government does not own massive fleets of trucks and buses that are designated for use when disaster strikes. Buying and maintaining such fleets in several locations throughout the nation would be far too costly. Instead, it was our job to keep track of where necessary vehicles could be obtained from the private sector. We would authorize the hiring of trucks and drivers who would then haul the supplies as required.

The civilian contractors were necessary but not ideal. During the time I was Under Secretary of Homeland Security (and, I understand, in the years before my appointment), there was a recurring problem. The contractors were hired and dispatched only when it was safe to begin moving into the affected area. However, traffic would be slow and no one knew what they would be facing when they reached the affected areas. After Hurricane Katrina had passed through truckers approaching the area would use their CB radios to learn what was happening a mile or two down the road. That was when we discovered that the drivers were reporting unconfirmed rumors.

"We heard there was rioting in the Superdome."

"We heard a truck was mobbed, overturned, and the supplies stolen from it."

"We heard . . ."

None of the rumors were based in fact, but the truckers, frightened by the unknown, made matters worse as they scared one another with unconfirmed reports. Worse, if they turned on whatever local radio station was broadcasting, the on-air reporters would sometimes repeat the same rumors. They rarely had a professional journalist reporting what he or she was seeing. Instead they would have people calling in with rumors, or they would interview people who "knew someone" who had seen shootings, gang violence, or whatever other horror they imagined.

If the truckers believed what they were reporting to one another, the drivers would frequently pull into a rest stop or move to the side of the highway and wait until they could determine how safe it was to keep driving. Invariably they eventually reached their destinations, but their journey was slower because of the rumors.

The second resource involved urban search and rescue (USAR) teams. Thirty-eight teams were spread around the country when I was part of the system, with each team comprising specialists from city and county departments. They might include firefighters, paramedics, police, and others. They are all civilian employees of their departments, spending their days handling local problems. However, throughout the year they come together periodically for special training. They are also provided with special equipment and trained to use it, such as biohazard clothing. Like the truckers, the USAR teams are called together when there is a disaster, then rush to the area where they assemble and wait until the problem has abated enough for them to move in.

The USAR teams are small, perhaps eighteen to twenty men and women at the most when I was involved. They have been trained to divide the affected area into grids and then work in a manner that ensures that everyone trapped can be located as quickly as possible. There may be four or five or more USAR teams working a disaster, and though their numbers are small, they coordinate with other rescue workers, such as the U.S. Coast Guard, to make sure that no one is missed.

I quickly learned to ignore the problems that were outside of the control of my departments and the agencies I worked with. All we could do with our Hurricane Pam simulation was assure ourselves that when a governor issued a cry for help, everything was in order to meet that need.

THE DIRTY LITTLE SECRET OF DISASTER PLANNING

On February 4, roughly five months before the creation of Hurricane Pam, I realized that all the priorities relative to homeland security were skewed at best, unrealistic at worst.

The problem was that the United States had been attacked by terrorists on September 11, 2001, an action that affected everyone's thinking. The incidents on that day were terrifying. The United States has been blessed to be physically isolated from enemies by a combination of the oceans off our east and west coasts, and friendly countries to the north and the south. We have a geographic "fort," if you will. It always seemed that an enemy would have to either use a guided missile whose flight we could track and hopefully destroy in the air, or penetrate our borders with enough personnel and equipment to attack our cities. Border security has always, in my opinion, been an issue of national security, not an issue of racism or prejudice or bigotry. There have been occasional teams of violent individuals, such as the Libyan hit squads known to be operating in California during part of Reagan's term. Earlier, during World War II, several Nazis entered the country after traveling by U-boat (German submarines). But other than the British invasion of the United States in 1812, we have been spared domestic attack. And though American property—embassies, hotels, and manufacturing plants—has been attacked abroad, the first time Americans felt vulnerable was on 9/11. Instead of looking at the real dangers facing themselves, their neighbors, and their country, they looked only at the extremists whose actions were limited. We were looking to defend ourselves against the relatively rare human assault and became increasingly indifferent in our policies and priorities to the major risks predictably facing our nation *every day.*

* * *

Journal entry for February 4, 2004:

> *I just had an under secretaries' meeting yesterday that was fascinating in what it revealed about so many different aspects of the department, from the personal characteristics of some of the people involved, to the utter disarray the department is creating among the components that are supposed to integrate into one.*
>
> *I have continually preached that the "all hazards" approach is the only way to effectively ensure that we are prepared not only for terrorist attacks (which, if law enforcement does its job, the number of attacks would be theoretically zero) but for any disaster that might occur. This is the FEMA approach that has worked for so many years, and was clearly successful in both the 1995 bombing of the Murrah Building and in the 2001 attacks on the World Trade Center and the Pentagon. As such I believe that "all hazards" should be the focus of the department, while recognizing that another directorate, such as Information Analysis & Infrastructure Protection, might conceivably be focused solely on terrorism.* [However, I can make a

strong argument that even this directorate has a role to play in the all-hazards approach. For example, it would easily be involved in an analysis of the vulnerabilities of infrastructure to any hazard.]

But alas, all hazards is not the focus of the department, and that was made abundantly clear this week in Admiral Loy's reaction to Roger Mackin's, the drug enforcement czar, report on drug seizures and the resultant decrease in drug money going to terrorist organizations. Ridge had asked the group to give examples of how we had made the country safer. In response, Roger stated that a record amount of cocaine had been seized. Loy immediately responded that those seizures weren't "terrorist related" so that wasn't what the secretary was interested in being able to report. Roger responded that drug money often goes to terrorist organizations, including Hezbollah, and as such, did have a role in terrorism.

The point is that Loy thinks that the focus of the department should be terrorism. What a mistake. Since September 2001, we have had no incidents of foreign terrorism on American soil. The anthrax attacks? Probably a domestic criminal. The ricin letters of this week? Probably related to a political issue of trucking regulations, not Al Qaeda. But, since 9/11, we have had a record tornado season, an incredibly expensive hurricane devastate parts of the East Coast, wildfires which destroyed 3,500 structures and burned more than 750,000 acres. So Mother Nature continues her terrorist attacks, but the Department of Homeland Security shows little interest. Unless, of course, you count Ridge's interest in a photo op after a disaster.

Unfortunately my thinking was prescient, not an achievement to feel proud about, for my fears meant that a portion of the country was radically changed for the worst, perhaps forever. I continue:

If this trend continues, they will decimate FEMA and the emergency management structure in this country. For example, emergency management planning grants are being subsumed into terrorist block grants to states. Governors will wrap that money *up in "homeland security" language and use it for things other than a robust emergency management system in their states. Then, when the next natural disaster strikes, they won't be able to handle it. Assistance to Firefighter Grants are being subsumed by the Office of Domestic Preparedness, which has no infrastructure to support over 20,000 grants totaling $750 million. They put out about 15 grants per year, all in blocks, not done competitively, and not audited. So the nest time a fire strikes San Diego or San Bernardino County, the firefighters won't be ready for urban wild land interface fires, but they'll be ready for an anthrax attack.*

My personal journal further explained one other reaction to external danger, this time related to airlines. Remember that at the same time that we were looking at how to best handle natural disasters, the nation, and that includes the leaders of both government and business, was still concerned about terrorist attacks involving aircraft. In an entry that immediately followed the issue of natural disaster danger versus the crises caused by enemies, I wrote:

The newest tool we're using to fight terrorism is the cancellation of airline flights. Starting at Christmas, there was supposedly intelligence of a specific nature that terrorists had targeted specific airlines (Air France and British Airways) flying into the United States. So flights were cancelled by the airlines well in advance. Duh, so we give the terrorists knowledge that we know what they're targeting, the flights get cancelled, the terrorists drive away from the airport or just never show up, and we've done nothing to solve the long-term problem. In fact, we've probably exacerbated it by revealing the information that we know of specific flights.

British Airways Flight 233 was cancelled several times. We revealed again this past weekend that specific intelligence targeted that same flight, and it was again cancelled. Doesn't anyone suspect that perhaps Al Qaeda is testing our intelligence system? Seeing what we know, perhaps putting guinea pigs out to see if we find them? Perhaps even toying with us while targeting specific flights that we cancel and then they're on another flight we don't know about? Just curious!

Last night at dinner, General [John] Gordon tells me we dodged a bullet on those cancellations. He described the intelligence as the equivalent of finding a hotel room with the words "British Airways" and "Flight 233" and "anthrax" and "bomb" written on pieces of paper, but in different piles, not necessarily connected, and perhaps even worse, deliberately put there. And so we cancel and now they know how or where we're tracking them.

My suggestion, which he agreed with but said the airlines themselves are the impediment, is to let the targeted plane load, act normal, taxi out as if ready to take off, and then announce a mechanical problem, take the plane to a corner of the airport, secure it, check it, and screen and interview all the passengers. If they planned to bomb or infect the plane, you have them cornered, you have them caught, we win, they lose.

To my surprise and consternation, John says the airlines oppose this idea. They don't want, for competitive reasons, to cancel flights at the last minute, but as early as possible so they can reclaim those passengers and get them on their company's other flights. I understand that, but in this case, if we have credible evidence, shouldn't the airlines show some patriotism and be willing to suffer a little loss to prevent another 9/11 which cost them billions?

John also says that the fear of the government is the site of a plane cornered, and the terrorists still release anthrax. To which I say, this is a war. And I thought we were telling everyone that anthrax was treatable? What if it was smallpox? Same thing; we keep telling people that they can get vaccinated up to 48 hours after exposure. Well, we vaccinate them on the spot. What if it's chemical? We might lose passengers, but again, this is a war. How many people lost their lives in World War II trying to preserve freedom and liberty? So far, 3,000 in NYC gave their lives and over 500 soldiers in Iraq have given their lives. Perhaps one more plane would save untold thousands if we break up their organization by using these tactics. Otherwise, they continue to play us, we go broke, and they still attack.

It was obvious that misguided fear and indifference was guiding what we were trying to do. Fortunately, at the time I made my entries and later when we conducted our exercise with Hurricane Pam, we were still able to look at disasters in a way that prepared us for a situation where everyone—the governors, mayors, first responders, and the public at large—acted in ways they understood and could be most effective. What I did not anticipate were the delays caused by too many people considering whether NIMBI should be added to the last-minute planning. And as too often is the case, men and women in positions of authority stopped to think whether an action was in their best interest and by then real life had made the decision for them.

* * *

Journal entry for April 17, 2004. Quote of opening statement by Congressman Hal Rogers (R-KY), chair of the subcommittee overseeing FEMA's appropriations, who was outraged over Tom Ridge's attempt to dismantle FEMA:

> *"This morning we welcome the Under Secretary for Emergency Preparedness and Response, Michael Brown. Secretary Brown, I welcome you back for your second appearance before this subcommittee. As the Director of FEMA, your mission is to reduce loss of life and property and protect our nation's critical infrastructure from all types of hazards through a comprehensive, risk-based, emergency management program of mitigation, preparedness, response and recovery. In many ways, your directorate is the first to respond to a national emergency or disaster. It was FEMA who led the Federal response and recovery efforts to the September 11th terrorist attacks. And it will be FEMA who continues to be there after every disaster, whether natural or manmade, to help the nation recover.*
>
> *"It has been one year since FEMA became part of the Department of Homeland Security, yet there continues to be restructuring. Programs you inherited just last year are now being transferred back out. The Strategic National Stockpile is moving back to the Department of Health and Human Services, while the Metropolitan Medical Response System is being transferred*

within the Department. In addition, several traditional FEMA grant programs, such as the Emergency Management Performance Grants and Firefighter Assistance Grants, have recently been moved to a new Office of State and Local Government Coordination and Preparedness. I am sure you are anxious for some stability.

"Your agency has always championed an all hazards approach to preparedness. Yet I am beginning to worry about the future of all hazards planning. Despite Homeland Security Presidential Directive-8, which calls for an all-hazards approach, despite the fact that these grants are no longer under your jurisdiction. FEMA is built on a history of all hazards planning, response, and recovery, and I am curious to hear your plans to ensure the Department continues that focus.

"Over the past year we have seen devastating wildfires in California and a major hurricane strike the east coast. In fact, in FY [fiscal year] 2003 you responded to over 120 declared disasters and emergencies. We worked with you to be sure that, when additional funding was needed to respond to disasters, it was there. Hurricane researchers are predicting another year with above average activity. Rest assured that we will continue to work with you and provide the resources you need to respond to these disasters and provide recovery assistance."

If we had only known . . .

CHAPTER 5

HURRICANE CHARLEY, OUR BAPTISM BY FIRE

AUGUST 13, 2004: When Hurricane Charley struck the Gulf Coast on Friday the 13th, I felt like a soldier who had just completed basic training and was immediately dropped into the middle of a combat zone. Were all the months of preparation adequate for what we were facing? Had we planned for the full range of problems we would confront? Had we trained others well enough so we could work as a cohesive team, the group more effective than any one individual?

In hindsight a year later, we all realized that Katrina was the storm we thought Charley was going to be. Not that it would have made any difference. Past experience and the Hurricane Pam exercise had prepared us for a national response as much as possible without facing the real thing. It also helped that Florida was probably the most experienced and best prepared of all the states along the Gulf Coast when it came to enduring and responding to hurricanes.

The basic concerns were clear from the moment the tropical storm morphed into a Category 4 storm that had wind surges reaching 145 miles an hour when it struck west-central Florida at Charlotte Harbor. One seemingly safe shelter holding twelve hundred people had its roof blown off. Sixteen people were found dead shortly after it struck, an unknown number of others were missing and thousands more made homeless. Trees were snapped in half, power lines were down, and the preliminary damage was believed to be in excess of $15 billion.

Adding to the stress of handling the disaster was the fact that the *Wall Street Journal* had assigned reporter Bobby Block to follow me for the previous couple of months. The paper wanted to do a story about me, FEMA, and whether the new Homeland Security umbrella had reduced the ability of FEMA to effectively respond. As I told Bobby when he asked about whether I felt pressure to handle the emergency, "I feel under pressure to perform at every disaster because I have seen the faces of the people who have suffered. . . . It doesn't make any difference where this was. . . . I do think we need to show that FEMA knows what it's doing."

There was seemingly extra pressure with Charley because Florida, whose governor, Jeb Bush, was the President's brother, would be watched closely by our critics. Would everyone get the help they needed in a timely manner? Would Florida residents get more than others? Faster than others? Or would all areas struck by Charley receive quality support?

The *Wall Street Journal* reporter was also concerned with the priority politics within FEMA that were being experienced in the aftermath of Charley. I and others had explained that we were looking at two different missions. One was to prevent terrorism, an essentially proactive law enforcement concern. The second was to prepare the country for all hazards. This was also my personal sense of the mission assigned to us.

The attacks on September 11 resulted in a reduction in federal funding for state emergency managers who were concerned with preparation to deal with natural catastrophes. The money taken from natural disaster response, along with additional funds, was authorized for counterterrorism. By the time Charley struck the Gulf Coast, antiterrorism spending was more than $3 billion, up from just $221 million in 2001 when the 9/11 attacks occurred. And FEMA's grant money meant for state and local emergency management had been reduced by a third, to $180 million. But our real test of the moment, the one that ultimately helped prepare us for Katrina, came in the aftermath of Hurricane Charley when I worked closely with Jeb Bush, whose state was hit hardest.

The basic work was relatively simple because Jeb and his state's staff had been dealing with these crises several times a year. Charley was unusual in its strength, but the needs of the people in the affected areas were no different than in the past. A joint command was established with Craig Fugate, then the manager for Florida's state emergency. Jeb and I sat down with our respective people on the ground, one from Florida and one from FEMA. We immediately divided up responsibilities so that no one overlapped and no need was missed. We didn't need the new Department of Homeland Security's resources or involvement. We also didn't need a show of politics, but that was exactly what Secretary Tom Ridge provided as the rest of us were doing the necessary work, as I noted in my journal the week following Hurricane Charley:

Of course Secretary Ridge had to come down. The best story about Ridge's visit was during our drive to visit a disaster recovery center [DRC] in Lee County (Ft. Myers, I think). On the way there, he has a motorcade that is at least as big as the President's, and why, I don't know. [President Bush had flown into Fort Myers to meet with his brother and myself in order to tour the affected area. This was done before Ridge arrived.] *But driving along a commercial street, four lanes wide, I see three little children dart into the center median. The oldest couldn't be ten, and the other two much younger. I'm fearing they're going to dart into the path of the motorcade, so brace myself for what I assume is going to be hard braking. Stupid me. What does the motorcade do? Blare their sirens at them! All I could think of was how it would look had Ridge's motorcade hit one of those kids, especially after the sirens scared them and they ran into the path of the cars. It was ridiculous.*

The second great story about his visit occurred after we had driven through a pretty deserted neighborhood that had already moved most of their debris into the curb area, cleaned their homes up, and gone back to work. The neighborhood was deserted. We got to the end of a street and lo-and-behold, a pickup truck with a couple of workers. So Ridge asks the drivers to stop, gets out and talks to this guy for fifteen minutes while the press corps following him gets some shots. We get back in the car and continue on to the DRC. As we approach the DRC he asks who did the advance work for the President, and I tell him, of course, that White House advance teams did it. He then asks, rhetorically, I wonder who picked these places for me? He was clearly irritated that he wasn't getting the same treatment as the President, and I'm thinking, there's really no need for you to be here anyway.

Between those seeking photo ops while seemingly indifferent to the suffering and the careful coordination of resources within a state familiar with natural disasters, my work in Florida in the aftermath of Hurricane Charley gave me both an education and a warning about what could happen. It would be months before I could put what I learned fully into practice, and that event started with the benign name Tropical Depression 12.

CHAPTER 6

DISASTER POLITICS

HOW A NATURAL disaster is handled can become a matter of national politics. Manmade disasters, such as the destruction of the World Trade Towers, require very little response from politicians in order to look good. The mayor and perhaps the governor go to the site of the destruction. They decry the loss of life. They stress that the city is tougher than any enemy. They pledge to rebuild, to make the city greater than before.

The President also comes to the site of a manmade disaster, this time with anger in his voice and, if he is either deeply moved or a good actor, perhaps with a tear in his eye. He announces that the people who caused the crisis will be hunted down and destroyed. It does not matter where in the world they try to hide. America is greater than such cowards and the army is already making plans to go on the attack. Re-election campaigns will carry footage of whoever appeared at the site. There will be a flag flying, the embrace of first responders and volunteer rescue workers, and appropriate music.

A natural disaster is another matter. The public perception is that there is enough time to protect lives and property. The average citizen has no idea what preparations were made or could have been made. Maybe the average citizen either lived through it or, more likely, watched it on television and recognized the overwhelming force of nature. The problem is that reality is no more important with a natural disaster than a manmade one, the only difference is the expectation that the former will result in immediate, rapid cleanup and recovery efforts since there was time to anticipate the problem, and the latter will result in a coming together of experts and average citizens to plan a slower, albeit just as thorough, response.

In the months prior to Katrina, Florida was struck by four hurricanes and George Bush's reelection campaign. When I read outside analyses of the events and what amounted to my role in it all, I realized that saving careers had become almost as important as saving lives. As Charles Mahtesian, editor of *Almanac of American Politics*, explained in his article "How FEMA Delivered Florida for Bush":

> It is almost impossible to overstate the political importance of Florida, the fourth biggest election prize, with 27 electoral votes. In 2000, when Bush and Democratic nominee Al Gore battled to a 49 percent draw in the state, the official recount that gave Bush a 537-vote win also gave him the presidency. In 2004, both presidential campaigns targeted Florida with an intensity that assumed the state would be just as competitive as four years before.
>
> Neither party, however, could have foreseen the role that Mother Nature would play. Beginning in August, Florida was flattened by four successive hurricanes that ripped up broad swaths of the state. Between hurricanes Charley, Frances, Ivan and Jeanne, the storm damage was estimated to run as high as $26 billion.
>
> In 1992, the last time a major hurricane pummeled Florida in the homestretch of a presidential election, FEMA was caught with its pants down. Its response to Hurricane Andrew was disorganized and chaotic, leaving thousands without shelter and water. Cleanup and resupply efforts were snarled in red tape. After watching the messy relief efforts unfold, lawmakers questioned whether FEMA was a Cold War relic that ought to be abolished. . . .
>
> In 2004, George W. Bush and FEMA left little room for error. Not long after Hurricane Charley first made landfall on Aug. 13, Bush declared the state a federal disaster area to release federal relief funds. Less than two days after Charley ripped through southwestern Florida, he was on the ground touring hard-hit neighborhoods.

Bush later made a handful of other Florida visits to review storm-related damage, but the story on the ground was not Bush's hand-holding. Rather, it was FEMA's performance.

Charley hit on a Friday. With emergency supply trucks pre-positioned at depots for rapid, post-storm deployment, the agency was able to deliver seven truckloads of ice, water, cots, blankets, baby food and building supplies by Sunday. On Monday, hundreds of federal housing inspectors were on the ground, and FEMA already had opened its first one-stop disaster relief center.

By the end of September, three hurricanes later, the agency had processed 646,984 registrations for assistance with the help of phone lines operating 24 hours a day, seven days a week. Fifty-five shelters, 31 disaster recovery centers and six medical teams were in operation across the state. Federal and state assistance to households reached more than $361 million, nearly 300,000 housing inspections were completed, and roughly 150,000 waterproof tarps were provided for homeowners, according to FEMA figures.

It's impossible to know just how much of an effect FEMA had on the Florida vote. Many of the citizens the agency served there presumably had more important things to worry about. It's also hard to imagine that, even with its shock-and-awe hurricane response, a bureaucracy like FEMA pleased all its customers. Even so, in a closely contested state where hundreds of thousands of voters suffered storm-related losses, it's equally hard to imagine that they didn't notice the agency's outreach. (*National Journal*, November 3, 2004)

I read the article with two reactions. The first was with delight because it was personally flattering. Some of the readers who commented on the piece felt that FEMA employees were "just doing their job." But regardless, FEMA was recognized for what it did, and I knew how bad it could have been for the President had we screwed up Florida.

The second reaction was a sense of vindication because we handled the Florida disasters after insisting that the Department of Homeland Security stay out of our way while we responded.

Later that month, during a meeting with Andy Card in the West Wing of the White House, the political side of disaster response was again mentioned. "How does it feel to be responsible for having saved this presidency?" Andy asked as his deputy chief of staff, Joe Hagin, watched.

I was astonished and told him so. I told him that was the greatest compliment anyone had paid me for the work we did in Florida with the hurricanes just before the election. I demurred slightly and told him that what we really did was prevent Florida from becoming a fiasco for the President, but that I appreciated his way of saying it a lot better! My head was huge at that point.

There were internal politics involved in the disaster work. Karl Rove had never been a fan of mine. Years after I left the government, after George Bush was no longer in office, Karl wrote a book that was as unflattering to me as his original opposition. However, during the Allbaugh's Christmas party for 2004, he spotted me, shook my hand, then bowed and gesticulated, saying, "Your eminence! Your eminence!" He then proceeded to tell my wife, Tamara, that his greatest professional accomplishment was "advocating strongly for the nomination of Mike Brown as undersecretary at DHS," and laughing out loud as he did it. He knew full well that he had done just the opposite. Rove had opposed my nomination as the Under Secretary of Homeland Security. He lost that battle to Clay Johnson, the head of the transition team setting up the new department. However, the Florida disaster work had gotten through his bias against me, forced him to look at what we had achieved and the fact that the President probably owed his reelection to the votes the Florida effort had given him. What I did not consider and probably should have was the fact that if he were quick to praise someone whose appointment he had worked hard to block, he would be just as comfortable throwing me away regardless of my accomplishments when a scapegoat was needed.

CHAPTER 7

ANTICIPATION BECOMES REALITY

A **UGUST 24, 2005:** The weather system was called Tropical Depression 12, a term used by meteorologists to identify the strength of a minor storm. For me, it was a short-lived name. The wind picked up, the rain gained in intensity, and Mother Nature gave birth to Tropical Storm Katrina as it raced to the Central Bahamas. Then, as it continued moving toward the southeastern Florida coast, Tropical Storm Katrina became Hurricane Katrina and our July 2004 exercise morphed into an expected but unwanted reality.

I gathered the people necessary to implement whatever rescue and relief would be needed, some in the same office, most scattered around the country though connected through videoconferencing. New Orleans would become our ultimate concern, of course. It was the city that had always been in the greatest danger. But there was no predicting with certainty that New Orleans would bear the brunt of the storm. What we knew for certain was that Florida would be struck first, a fact understood by Florida governor Jeb Bush who was the first U.S. official to call on the federal government for immediate help.

Florida was an easy state for us to begin putting our preparations into effect. Longtime residents and relative newcomers who had the sense to listen to the instructions of old-timers stockpiled flashlights, water, canned goods, boards, nails, duct tape, and whatever else they would need to secure their residences and businesses. They had learned which storms they could ride out and which would require evacuation. They knew time constraints, escape routes, and had the sense to leave their homes in time to reach safe areas when the more severe storms were approaching.

The governor's office also had no illusions about what was taking place. Governor Bush, like his predecessors, regularly did disaster planning. There would be no panic. There would be no delays. We had already been through four hurricanes in the previous year, and while I could not imagine new problems arising, any that did would be presumably only minor variations of past events.

* * *

August 25, 2005: Hurricane Katrina reached Category 1 status while we watched it move west at 80 miles per hour. We did not rush personnel into the areas we thought would receive the greatest damage. We did not send a convoy of trucks filled with emergency supplies racing across the nation. Instead we quietly waited. A natural disaster cannot be stopped, cannot be slowed, and cannot be diverted. It will strike where nature takes it. It will destroy what it destroys, and leave untouched what it fails to damage, and there is no human logic to identify why one building or city is flattened and another, facing the same force of wind and rain, is not. We were set to respond to any reality as we had in the recent past.

Governor Jeb Bush understood all the FEMA and Homeland Security procedures; he always followed the course of the hurricane until it struck the coast and he could declare a state of emergency. Then he requested immediate help from us, understanding that we would begin moving personnel and supplies to the affected area but wouldn't enter any location until the storm moved past. This was not because he was the President's brother or that he belonged to the same political party. Disaster planning and disaster response were part of the thinking for every governor of Florida because, given its location, it would always be in danger.

A Category 1 hurricane does not seem that bad. The wind force is often no greater than the impact of a car crash where two vehicles each traveling at 40 miles an hour hit head-on. Many such accidents leave the vehicles wrecked but the drivers unhurt, the airbags providing full protection.

Try to cross a street when the wind is striking you at 80 miles per hour and you will likely be knocked off your feet or thrown against a building. High-profile vehicles such as SUVs can become sails in the wind, the drivers unable to steer effectively. Mobile home parks look like they were struck by bombs. Flying shards of glass become as deadly as knives thrown by a martial artist.

This still "minor" Hurricane Katrina struck Florida at 7 p.m. All responders were prepared yet nine Floridians were killed almost immediately. The next day would be worse.

* * *

August 26, 2005: As we expected from our exercise involving Hurricane Pam, Hurricane Katrina's wind speed momentarily dropped to 75 miles an hour by 9 a.m. The change was not as encouraging as it might seem. It was like a long-distance runner slowing briefly around the curve before increasing speed for an all-out race to the finish, in this case Louisiana. And, as our experts predicted, eight hours later the storm had regained its momentum and became a Category 2. Hurricane Katrina was now ripping along the gulf at 100 miles per hour.

Hurricane Katrina swept through Florida, traveled along the Gulf Coast, and continued picking up speed. Unless it shifted direction, it would strike New Orleans with a minimum speed of 115 miles per hour—Category 3. The mayor knew this. The governor knew this. The city's first responders, along with first responders in those nearby communities that maintained mutual assistance pacts, knew this. That was why we expected the same call for assistance Jeb Bush had made. That was why we also expected a mandatory evacuation order within New Orleans. Instead I felt we were confronted with denial, delay, and poor choices.

The White House recognized there was an impending disaster for the entire Gulf Coast region and ordered all of us in FEMA and the Department of Homeland Security (DHS) to prepare. We had been in regular contact with the mayors and governors of the areas likely to be affected. We were constantly updating the President. In addition, where possible, plans were being made to utilize the National Guard to supplement the USAR teams, local and state law enforcement officers, and other regional first responders.

Remember that the President was not in a position to order the National Guard into an area, only to approve the cost and provide essential supplies when the governors requested them. Some areas, such as Florida where ten thousand men and women were called up to help, were able to immediately activate their units. Other areas had National Guard units that were no longer in the state. They had been called to active duty and were on the ground in Iraq and other international trouble spots. Each governor was aware of his or her resources as the hurricane approached.

Louisiana's National Guard was almost half its usual strength. Four thousand men and women were available for service within the state; of a normal force of seven thousand, three thousand had been sent to Iraq along with critical equipment including high-water vehicles. I was not aware of the latter at the time, but news reports from both Louisiana publications and some of the national news organizations mentioned the high-water equipment.

* * *

Looking back, I feel that NIMBI politics intruded on common sense. Louisiana governor Kathleen Blanco was said to dislike New Orleans mayor Ray Nagin. She had the legal right to declare a state of emergency, to arrange for disaster assistance, and to bring federal resources to bear even as the hurricane was still approaching the coast. Instead, since it was increasingly clear that New Orleans would bear the brunt of the storm, she let Mayor Nagin make the final decision about seeking assistance. And both of them seemed to believe that being first with decisive action was not in their best interest. A mistake might be made that a delay could prevent.

The problem was Hurricane Katrina. Natural disasters do not consider the interests of anyone. The governor's decision to act only after the mayor requested her to do so might be politically appropriate—recognizing that the mayor's responsibilities were greater at that moment than the state's—but it turned problems considered difficult, though still possible to prevent, into ones that were unavoidable.

At 1:30 p.m. the governor and local officials in the state's endangered areas went on television to advise people to evacuate. This announcement was made with a lack of urgency considering that this region had experienced many storms in the past. The populace saw riding out a hurricane as giving them bragging rights; they were never told how serious Katrina was likely to be.

We wanted Mayor Nagin to order the mandatory evacuation of New Orleans, a critical concern in order to save lives. Some residents were not in denial and left the city well ahead of Katrina. Many more did not, and among those who stayed were people without cars, the sick, and the infirm. They would need special assistance both to leave the city and also, for some, when they arrived at a designated shelter. And the longer the mayor waited, the longer it took for the governor to make a request for help, which meant less could be done to help people before the storm hit.

Adding to the problem was the lack of accurate information coming from both the mayor's and the governor's offices, as well as my agency's inability to take the time to educate the media about what could and could not be accomplished. Many in the press thought that what was taking place was little different from a military operation. They assumed that whatever the city needed would instantly be provided either from our nonexistent FEMA holdings of buses, trucks, and so on, or from the military forces just waiting to pour into the city the same way they had gone to Baghdad. One story told of the governor's office demanding seven hundred buses for *immediate* evacuation of the New Orleans residents who had no other way to leave. That was all—seven hundred buses. We had to explain that they did not exist, that we would cover the cost of any that could be rented though it was probably too late for an effective evacuation. (The buses we eventually authorized were for use after Katrina passed. Buses would have been effective in evacuating the city, but the mayor did not want to give the order. Once the storm hit, even knowing the location of such equipment became meaningless. You can't load people onto buses in the midst of a storm with horrific winds. The chance of severe injury or death was far greater than having to seek refuge in a less than perfect building like the Superdome.)

We had also tried to get Mayor Nagin to alert people that Amtrak agreed to provide free transportation on the trains it was taking out of town to prevent their damage in the storm. The airlines also announced that they would take on passengers as they moved their planes out of the city. So far as I know the airlines would have charged the passengers, but the important point was that there were resources ignored by local leaders right up until it was too late. By then my only recourse was to give as many cable television interviews as I could, telling people in the affected areas that if I lived there, I'd get my butt out of the city.

* * *

The *National Journal* is one of the most important and influential weekly publications you have probably never heard of, but it is must-reading in Washington, D.C. A regular feature is the daily updated Hot Line where the following appeared shortly after Katrina devastated New Orleans:

> Mayor Ray Nagin said he plans to order a mandatory evacuation for most hurricanes with Category 2 strength and above in the future, and the Superdome will no longer be available as a refuge of last resort. Nagin: "A mandatory evacuation will be called in the future, as we know the threats will be coming. We have direct lines in to the National Hurricane Center, and we will coordinate at the state and federal level to give enough time for our citizens to reach safety." Those without transportation would utilize the Regional Transit Authority buses; RTA drivers would be considered essential personnel.
>
> City emergency preparedness officials told state officials that they have only 80 buses to evacuate the estimated 10K people without transportation, and the city cannot guarantee drivers. Gov's Office of Homeland Security and Emergency Preparedness dir. Col. Jeff Smith: "The (state) Department of Transportation and Development is working with them to see what their shortage will be. We're diligently working to have contracts in place with other school systems and with commercial carriers to make up the distance."
>
> Nagin said residents choosing to stay in their homes despite the evacuation order will not be required to leave. Nagin: "We're dealing with adults. If you decide to disobey a mandatory evacuation and don't leave, you're confining yourself to your home

in an emergency. If you come outside and violate the curfew, you will be arrested." LG Mitch Landrieu (D): "I'm concerned that it took the mayor eight months to announce this plan. It's worth noting that this will be the mayor's fifth hurricane season. In 2004, Hurricane Ivan's near-miss exposed serious flaws with the city's plan for evacuation and shelter of last resort. These same issues haunted our city during Hurricane Katrina." (Mark Schleifstein, *New Orleans Times-Picayune*, May 3, 2006)

At 11 p.m. on August 26, Louisiana governor Kathleen Blanco, having been told that the storm would strike Gulfport and New Orleans if it did not veer from its present course, decided to declare a state of emergency. She did so after we had lost another day during which people could have been more easily evacuated.

Worse, neither the governor nor the news media understood how FEMA had to operate under the law and within the realities of the storm. We would not be sending people into the cities most likely to be struck in advance of the hurricane touching down. That would put first responders in danger; the people we needed most for rescue and recovery efforts could be killed or injured. Instead, when we got the required request to send federal assistance, the responders would be ordered to move toward the affected city but to remain outside the perimeter of the storm. They were to move closer only as Katrina moved farther away—usually a two- or three-day lag from the moment of activation.

* * *

I have determined that this incident is of such severity and magnitude that effective response is beyond the capabilities of the State and affected local governments, and that supplementary Federal Assistance [is needed] to save lives, protect property, public health, and safety, or to lessen or avert the threat of a disaster.

—Governor Kathleen Blanco

Specifically, FEMA is authorized to identify, mobilize, and provide at its discretion equipment and resources necessary to alleviate the impacts of the emergency.

—White House statement in response

The White House approval of the requests by the Louisiana and Mississippi governors meant that we immediately alerted them that they could do whatever was necessary to protect the people in their states. We, the federal government, would reimburse them for the expense.

The costs of a hurricane are usually measured by destroyed property. That was not our concern. Instead property damage was the nightmare for the insurance industry, the private businesses that would eventually pay based on the policies held by home and business owners. Property damage is usually not an expense for the state or federal government.

Instead, the region incurred the expenses most people overlook because they are not as dramatic as the collapse of a multimillion-dollar building. For example, law enforcement officers, emergency medical personnel, city bus drivers, and other critical personnel began working overtime—that high, unanticipated cost shattered annual budget plans and available funds. Then there was money spent for special equipment such as water rescue vehicles obtained from the Louisiana Department of Wildlife.

Another large expense was for the state police and the state highway department as they set up what is called a contra-flow. This is the re-routing of all traffic out of the cities being evacuated. The effort requires everything from police handling the movement of traffic to ensure an orderly exodus to highway workers putting up the signs needed for people to know where they are supposed to go. Everyone would likely be on overtime and the cost would be enormous. It was these costs that we assured the governor we would cover. It was our incentive to make certain the state's leaders did everything they needed to do without hesitation, knowing that when this was over we would cut a check to reimburse them. Under normal circumstances, FEMA reimburses only 75 percent of the cost of assistance. However, in a catastrophic situation such as Katrina governors will receive 100 percent of all costs. It is the only way to ensure the safety of the people most affected.

The requests by the governors, approved immediately, allowed us to start moving the rescue teams, the trucks with meals ready to eat (MREs), and other critical supplies from the nearest supply area—Dallas in this case—to the cities closest to the expected impact area.

There were thirty-eight urban search and rescue teams, and, at the time of Katrina, each team had eighteen members all coming from different city fire departments within the states where they were based. These men and women were considered FEMA "assets" but not FEMA employees. They were part of local units that became subject to FEMA only during times of activation. Previously they would have received special training and equipment from FEMA and practiced working as a team under disaster conditions. Selection is obviously an honor for the men and women, and proof of the skills they have honed at their regular jobs. However, again there is a cost. The teams have to be transported by the fastest available resource, not the cheapest. This may mean getting on a bus or commercial airline. This may mean chartering a private or military jet. At the same time, the communities they are leaving have to arrange for overtime and special coverage so their communities remain safe without some of their top people.

The team members and their home departments have to be assured they will be compensated in a timely manner. Any doubts in the minds of the mayors or governors could lead to delays in getting the most qualified individuals to the most critical areas.

* * *

August 27, 2005: It is one thing to say that we were ready to provide resources to New Orleans and quite another to say we were certain our preparedness would matter. The time to evacuate New Orleans had mostly passed. By 5 a.m. Hurricane Katrina's winds were 115 miles per hour (Category 3) and growing. We had been assured that the levees were built to withstand at least that strong a hurricane. What we never considered was that the original construction was only as effective as the regular maintenance those levees received, and in New Orleans the neglect of the levees had gone on for years. The Army Corps of Engineers that had built the levees had no idea if they were still adequate. Even more frightening was the fact that the hurricane's winds were taking the storm on a rollercoaster ride of speed, rushing to Category 4, pulling back to Category 3, and then picking up momentum once again. The indifference to necessary maintenance, the variable wind force, and the fact that residents had not been ordered from the city created what could become the greatest catastrophe in New Orleans's history.

Neither I nor any of my staff seemed able to convince the mayor and the governor of the extreme seriousness of delayed action. We had Max Mayfield, the director of the National Hurricane Center, call Mayor Nagin to explain why the approaching Katrina required immediate evacuation.

We used Mayfield because he was both an expert and an outsider. He was not political. He was not concerned with elections, the cost of crisis response, or anything else that impacted on city officials. He called to explain hurricanes in general and Katrina's movements in particular. He could say with certainty what would happen if the storm struck at Category 3 or higher and the city had not been evacuated. He asked Nagin to immediately order all residents to leave New Orleans.

The director's words had the weight of science. They did not have the weight of law. Instead, Mayor Nagin declared his city to be in a state of emergency and *suggested* that the residents *voluntarily* evacuate. He especially wanted the residents in the low-lying areas to leave. If they so chose. It was really up to them, though it would be a good idea.

* * *

At 7:30 a.m., a conference call took place in New Orleans. It did not involve me or President Bush, though Sandy Coachman of FEMA was a part of it. The conference was one of many held starting several days prior to Katrina striking the Gulf Coast. They were all coordinated from the Emergency Command Center in Baton Rouge, and the men and women who participated would repeat such conferences, updating one another, every three or four hours until the storm struck. These were not supposed to be made public. They had been recorded by a local official named Walter Maestri who eventually provided them to National Public Radio. It was only after the recordings were made public that it was possible for us to prove the accuracy of the statements we had been making about where problems occurred.

"I'm very concerned right now," said Mayor Nagin, "because if the governor and Aaron Broussard [Jefferson Parish president] or Ray Nagin go out at noon and start talking about evacuations, we are going to alert almost a million people to hit the road." [*Parish* is a European term that means "county." Louisiana is the only state in the United States that uses the term.]

Colonel Jeff Smith, deputy director of Louisiana's Office of Emergency Preparedness (Louisiana's emergency manager was under federal indictment and had been removed from office, another distraction to the state's emergency organization), explained that he thought the logistics could be worked out in the next few hours. However, when they had the next conference three hours later, there was great concern about finding shelters for people who were sick, especially those who depended on electrically powered oxygen tanks and dialysis machines. The need for properly equipped shelters had been discussed five years earlier, and though buildings had been identified, there were no generators available to run the machinery.

There were other concerns as well. The New Orleans Fire Department lacked even a single boat. There was also a lack of critical supplies to help the men and women who might be facing fires and explosions from broken natural gas pipelines and other secondary disasters. When complaints were made to the leadership, the complainers were considered alarmists.

By 9:30 p.m. Governor Blanco became a key part of the planning by video teleconference. She was aware that no evacuation order had been given; it was only suggested, mostly to those living at lower levels of the city, that residents might want to evacuate. She is quoted as saying,

> I want to emphasize the importance of getting as many people out as we possibly can. I mean, in the low-lying areas, we have to have near 100 percent evacuation. Now it occurred to me that a lot of people went to bed last night thinking the hurricane was going to Florida. If they've been busy all day with the children and stuff like that and haven't been by a TV or a radio, the chances are good that tonight, they're finding out about it for the first time. I think a lot of people will show up at their churches and ask them to let people say a few prayers, but tell them to go home and pack and get out. ("Conference Calls Detail Katrina Concerns, Failings," NPR, September 23, 2005)

* * *

By contrast with what was taking place in Louisiana, at 5 p.m. that Saturday Mississippi governor Haley Barbour declared a state of emergency for his state, and then ordered the mandatory evacuation of Hancock County. Hancock was the region where the storm was most likely to strike, with the greatest loss of life. At worst, it would do less damage than the potential destruction faced by New Orleans. At best, hindsight would prove the evacuation had been unnecessary. He did not care. His only focus was on saving lives; then he would provide whatever the residents needed during the recovery phase.

The contrast with New Orleans seemed almost surreal as Mayor Nagin suggested his constituents might wish to get out of the way of a hurricane that was probably fast approaching and might break the levees and could cause extensive flooding unless, of course, it veered or something. So, given the unknown, the evacuation was voluntary.

One hour after Governor Barbour and Mayor Nagin issued their radically different instructions concerning the same storm, the National Weather Service predicted that there was a 45 percent chance that New Orleans would be directly hit by either a Category 4 or Category 5 hurricane. Under the best of circumstances it was doubtful that the levees protecting New Orleans could handle such impact. However, there was still a 55 percent chance that Hurricane Katrina would pass New Orleans, or that the storm would be weaker than everyone's worst fears. It was that on which the mayor seemed to focus, recognizing that an ultimately unnecessary mandatory evacuation would have financial and political repercussions. Mayor Nagin did not change the voluntary evacuation statement. I remember being interviewed by a reporter from a cable news program around the same time, and I bluntly said that if I lived in New Orleans, I'd be getting my butt out of there right then.

* * *

August 28, 2005: Hurricane Katrina became a Category 4 hurricane at 2 a.m. Five hours later it was a Category 5, with winds of 160 miles an hour. So far as anyone knew, there were no structures in the city of New Orleans, including the levees, that had been built to withstand such an impact. If the force was sustained when it struck the city, New Orleans could be destroyed. Finally the mayor decided he had to act. Katrina's wind speed had reached 175 miles per hour. He told the governor that he needed her to activate all federal aid. And as would become tragically typical, both the mayor and the governor learned the price of delay.

* * *

We're facing the storm most of us have feared. This is going to be an unprecedented event.

—9:30 a.m. statement by Mayor Ray Nagin, quoted in the *New Orleans Times-Picayune*

We were briefing them way before landfall. . . . It's not like this was a surprise. We had in the advisories that the levee could be topped.

—frustrated rebuttal by Dr. Max Mayfield, as quoted in both the New Orleans newspaper and the *St. Petersburg Times*

I was outraged by what was happening in New Orleans. I felt that the mayor was playing political games. I don't think he was a bad man. I don't think he considered the consequences of putting political issues ahead of public safety. I just felt that he was so busy worrying about how he and the other local officials would be perceived that he made choices we had warned him against.

For example, on Sunday morning we learned that the mayor was meeting with the city's legal expert to see if the city would be liable for whatever happened during a mandatory evacuation. Sunday morning. It was a time when everything he might do from that time forward was either too late to be effective or would have negative results that could have been avoided. Katrina would make landfall in twenty hours. Experts on storms and evacuation had stated that at least double that time was necessary to evacuate New Orleans. The mayor had waited too long.

At 8 a.m. the New Orleans Superdome opened to the public. It was a dramatic gesture. The structure was familiar to sports fans throughout the United States. It was big, held thousands of people for every football game, and somehow seemed capable of defying the greatest of storms. There was the impression that if you could not flee the fury of nature, the Superdome would protect you from further harm. Unfortunately, this was not a facility properly equipped for those seeking shelter. It was not built to withstand the horrendous storm that was beginning to lash at the city. It was just the largest available facility close at hand for the people who learned too late that they should have left the city. With luck it might save lives. Unfortunately it was also twelve feet below sea level.

Nagin also announced twelve locations throughout New Orleans where anyone in need of transportation should begin lining up. The Regional Transit Authority (RTA) was sending buses on a route that would take them to the Superdome and other sites the mayor was quoted as calling "refuges of last resort."

I was angry. There should not have been any "last resort." Too much information had been available prior to when evacuation was no longer a realistic option. Everywhere else along the Gulf Coast evacuation orders had been posted. In New Orleans, Ray Nagin didn't order a mandatory evacuation until Sunday morning at 11 a.m. central time. The action was demanded by President Bush who also recognized the inadvertent negligence.

* * *

Video teleconferencing (VTC) is the modern version of the teleconference where a number of individuals come together by speaker phone for a "real time" discussion without the cost of travel. The White House utilizes VTC with special adaptations to make it secure from anyone who might try to hack into the system and listen in.

The nature of a disaster is such that VTC becomes a regular way for everyone involved to share information, including with the President who had yet to leave his Crawford, Texas, home. We utilized VTC extensively in the days just before Katrina made landfall in New Orleans; because the participants thought the audio and video recordings of the meetings would not be made public, as officials discovered their inactions resulted in deadly indifference, they went into classic CYA (cover your ass) mode. This included President Bush, who was a part of each of the VTCs, identifying himself by voice and also being visible on the video recordings.

On one conference held the day before Katrina reached New Orleans, I forcefully told both the President and my immediate boss, Michael Chertoff, "I'm concerned about . . . their ability to respond to a catastrophe within a catastrophe." I stated, "We're going to need everything that we can possibly muster, not only in this state and in the region, but the nation, to respond to this event." And because new problems had been created by all the delays, I told the government agencies involved to do whatever was necessary to help people, even if that meant bending the rules. "Go ahead and do it," I said. "I'll figure out some way to justify it. . . . Just let them yell at me."

Yet until the tapes were revealed in the months that followed and the full story publicized, there were misrepresentations at the highest level. For example, four days after New Orleans was all but destroyed in most sections of the city, the President stated, "I don't think anybody anticipated the breach of the levees." The statement contradicted Max Mayfield and made me look incompetent, and I took a lot of flack. There was nothing else to do. My immediate concern involved those affected by the storm in the four states that had felt the wrath of Katrina. I never expected the tapes taken of the conferences to be made public, and without them I would be seen as calling the President of the United States a liar at worst and unaware at best. Neither situation would convince my critics of the truth.

Ultimately I made the decision to physically give a copy of the videoconference to the Associated Press's Washington bureau chief, Ron Fournier. To this day I have mixed feelings about doing so. I felt that I needed to make clear what had happened. I do believe there are circumstances where the public needs information to be an informed electorate. And I was concerned that without the revelations the tape would provide, poor responses to disasters would continue. Perhaps only what has happened since in the relationship between government officials and disasters such as the BP oil spill truly justifies my action.

Some Louisiana officials claimed that the federal government was not prepared for the hurricane's touchdown. The statement was spread extensively by the media, usually without checking the facts. If the press did ask for a reaction from FEMA, all the official statement could say was that the Louisiana officials were mistaken. This was the classic he said–she said problem.

That Sunday videoconference ended at 4:40 p.m., and as a disgusted Congressman Thomas Davis III (R-VA) later said, "The president is still at his ranch, the vice president is still fly-fishing in Wyoming, the president's chief of staff is in Maine. In retrospect, don't you think it would have been better to pull together? They should have had better leadership. It's disengagement."

Maybe the critics were right. The problem every president faces is that there is a limit to what he can do. There is the appearance of leadership that comes with rushing to the area where a crisis has occurred and I think many people expect it. That certainly was the case with President Bush and it would prove to be the case with his successor, President Obama, during the early days of the BP oil spill. But when nothing meaningful can be done by the President, when all officials, first responders, and others are at work, strategies for dealing with the crisis in place and functioning effectively, what should the President do? Cancel a vacation? Cancel a golf game? President Jimmy Carter was notoriously famous for staying in the White House and working during the Iran hostage crisis, and he was criticized for trapping himself in the Oval Office, allegedly narrowing his perspective and ability to handle the crisis.

In New Orleans we had the marks. We had the breached levees. We had the broken levees. We had shelters that were inadequate. We had a mayor screaming for buses that never came even though he knew full well that he had ignored the school buses and other vehicles under his control in the days when evacuation was possible. He also was aware that the chain of command was such that he could not directly place an order for anything. The request had to come through Governor Blanco. But on March 1, 2006, months after the media attacks were forgotten by everyone except those of us who had been deeply hurt by the lies, copies of the VTCs from just before the landfall were discovered. The Associated Press and other news media played them on the air, and then posted copies on the Internet along with transcriptions. On them people like Colonel Jeff Smith, head of Louisiana's Office of Emergency Preparedness, a man who was well aware of on-the-ground needs and response preparations, said, "I think a lot of the planning FEMA has done with us the past year has really paid off."

* * *

At 3 p.m. cars were fleeing New Orleans at a rate of eighteen thousand per hour. Either in their own cars or with someone willing to take them, only 80 percent of the population of 485,000 was evacuating. Approximately 112,000 people had no access to transportation.

At 4 p.m. the National Weather Service alerted the country that it was increasingly likely New Orleans would be struck by a Category 4 or Category 5 hurricane. If that occurred, at least half the homes in the city would be seriously damaged. Homes with gabled roofs would be most susceptible. Power might be out for weeks. And water shortages would endanger everyone.

By 6 p.m. Ray Nagin was willing to order a curfew. Ten thousand people had reached the Superdome and 150 members of the National Guard were trying to keep those seeking refuge safe. An hour later there were reports that waves were crashing on the exercise path that had been built on the Lake Pontchartrain levee in Kenner, Louisiana. By morning the levee would be breached.

* * *

After a Sunday morning statewide conference call, I announced the first ever citywide Mandatory Evacuation order, opened the Louisiana Superdome as our refuge of last resort, staged buses throughout the city to transport people to the Superdome and set a curfew for dusk.

The City evacuated 400 special needs residents to a state shelter and then opened the Superdome at 8 a.m. for the remaining special needs population. . . .

On Monday, August 29, 2005 . . . thousands of people were stranded on their rooftops, or in attics, needing to be rescued. Hundreds died in the waters that engulfed our city. . . . Primary and secondary power sources, sewerage and draining systems and communication and power lines were incapacitated.

—Mayor Ray Nagin testifying on December 14, 2005,
before the U.S. House Select Committee to
Investigate the Preparation for and
Response to Hurricane Katrina

There were two opportunities to ensure an orderly evacuation of many of the residents who were ultimately trapped in New Orleans as Katrina ripped through the city. The city schools maintained a large fleet of buses normally used to transport children to and from their classes. These were parked, unused, and could easily have been pressed into service before the storm became too dangerous for driving.

In addition to the buses, Amtrak had a train that could hold several hundred people and it was leaving the city at 8:30 p.m. The use of the buses was the mayor's call. The use of the Amtrak train was an offer from a company willing to take as many people as possible out of harm's way. In both instances nothing was done. The empty train left the city and the buses stayed where they were parked.

Eventually Mayor Nagin addressed the issue when appearing on the NBC news show *Meet the Press* on September 11. He claimed that Amtrak never made the offer. In truth it had. The problem was that accepting the offer or using the buses would have meant the de facto declaration that the city had to be evacuated. Instead, Mayor Nagin avoided that issue until the next day, and by then it was too late.

* * *

I had another worry when even Louisiana officials expressed concern over the large number of residents who had not been evacuated. To my horror I noted that because of Mayor Nagin's refusal to order the evacuation in a timely manner, patients remained in hospitals dependent upon electricity that would quickly fail. Prisoners remained in their prisons. And tourists who had been living in hotels as the storm approached had also not been moved.

By nightfall it no longer mattered that most of our concerns had been ignored by the governor and the mayor. Flooding from the storm surges had begun and there was no way to fully protect New Orleans even if the levees held together. The levee that separates Lake Pontchartrain from New Orleans is 17.5 feet high. Other levees meant to keep out the waters the storm sent surging from the Gulf of Mexico are much lower. Experts watching the storm estimated that waters from the storm surge would rise to from 18 to 22 feet above normal tide levels. The water would likely carry waste products, toxic chemicals, and other contaminants making it unfit for human consumption. It would also be a carrier of infectious diseases.

We had our catastrophe within a catastrophe.

* * *

August 29, 2005: The disaster is in full force. The first reports indicate that Katrina made landfall along the Louisiana coast sometime after

6 a.m. with the force of a Category 4 hurricane—nearly 145 miles per hour. The speed would be somewhat less—a Category 3—when it reached New Orleans itself. Almost immediately the extent of the destruction reflected the poor condition of the levees and the fact that they had not been properly maintained, in some instances, for more than forty years.

The storm surge sent water up Lake Borgne and the lower sections of the Mississippi. The levees there were between 11 and 15 feet above sea level, but the storm surge topped them by another 5 to 10 feet. Worse, these were poorly constructed, already eroded earthen levees, though when the damage first occurred, both regional officials and the Army Corps of Engineers tried to claim that a barge had broken loose and caused the breach. Only months later would it be learned that a runaway barge had not been the problem. Barges and debris had struck the levee many times with no damage. Only years later would an investigation reveal the failure of the Army Corps of Engineers to provide proper maintenance. [To be fair, the Army Corps of Engineers could not act independently of the state government. There were allegations that at least some money was allocated for maintenance and that a portion of it was redirected for other regional needs, including the development of the offshore gambling casino activity.]

At 8 a.m. central time Mayor Nagin announced, "I've gotten reports this morning that there is already water coming over some of the levee systems. In the Lower Ninth Ward, we've had one of our pumping stations stop operating, so we'll have significant flooding. It is just a matter of how much." [There was 6 to 8 feet of water in the Lower Ninth Ward at the time.]

Slightly more than three hours later, the White House noted, "Flooding is significant throughout the region and a levee in New Orleans has reportedly been breached sending 6–8 feet of water throughout the 9th ward area of the city."

I arrived in Baton Rouge, the closest safe city to New Orleans, and called the President from my makeshift office in the Louisiana State Office of Emergency Preparedness. I explained that I did not know if the government had the capacity to respond to the way the catastrophe was unfolding within the catastrophe—what we thought was a Category 4 hurricane coupled with the thousands of people who had not left the area.

* * *

Hurricane Katrina, its 115–130 mph winds, and the accompanying storm surge it created as high as 27 feet along a stretch of the Northern Gulf Coast from Mobile, Alabama, to New Orleans, impacted nearly 93,000 square miles of our Nation—roughly an area the size of Great Britain. The disaster was not isolated to one town or city, or even one State. Individual local and State plans, as well as relatively new plans created by the Federal government since the terrorist attacks on September 11, 2001, failed to adequately account for widespread or simultaneous catastrophes.

We were confronted by the pictures of destroyed towns and cities, each with their own needs. Smaller cities like Waveland, Mississippi, were completely devastated by Hurricane Katrina and required smaller scale yet immediate search and rescue efforts as well as large volumes of life saving and sustaining commodities. New Orleans, the largest affected city—which dominated much of what Americans saw on their televisions— suffered first from the initial impact of Katrina and then from the subsequent flood caused by breaches in its 350 mile levee system. Over an estimated eighteen-hour period, approximately 80 percent of the city flooded with six to twenty feet of water, necessitating one of the largest search and rescue operations in our Nation's history.

—*Federal Response to Hurricane Katrina: Lessons Learned,*
White House document, February 2006

THE AUTOPEN FIASCO

While this catastrophe was taking place, I became the unwitting victim of an unknown bureaucrat trying to help all of us in Louisiana, though doing so from the FEMA headquarters in Washington and without my knowledge.

The problem was that wonderful device called an autopen. The autopen was developed so that celebrities, highly regarded business people, and others would be able to respond to autograph requests without wasting their time or hiring a staff to fake their signatures. The system used a real pen that put the same pressure on the paper as you do when handwriting a signature. This makes it difficult if not impossible for most people to tell what has been signed and what has been created with the autopen.

We periodically used an autopen for internal memos and special requests, but we had a procedure to follow. The autopen made it possible for an executive assistant to prepare a document, for example, and then sign it with the autopen as though his or her boss had actually seen it. Then the document would be sent to each person up the chain of command who would read it, then sign it in the normal fashion if approved. Ultimately this included the official whose autopen signature was at the bottom of the letter or document.

The idea worked well. Many of us were traveling almost constantly and the approach with the autopen seemed to be faster and more effective than trying to get everyone together at the same time. The problem arose, as we learned with Katrina, when there was a crisis and too many people were running around like chickens with their heads cut off.

Tuesday morning somebody in the FEMA office, I never did learn who it was, was requesting "bodies." FEMA had temporary employees called DAEs—disaster assistance employees. These are men and women who canvass neighborhoods immediately following a crisis. They are not search and rescue specialists. Rather they go to where people are safe but hurting. They may have lost critical possessions. They may have lost their homes and need a place to live. There could be any number of concerns, and it is the role of each DAE to talk with these people, learn their problems, and see how we can help them, including giving them the location of agencies with the resources they need. Their role is closer to that of what Red Cross personnel do when there is a fire in an apartment complex that suddenly leaves families without shelter. It is probably the most personal positive interaction Americans have with their government.

There is another side to the DAE work as well. The canvassers bring back information about the extent of neighborhood and infrastructure damage. They are on the ground, seeing everything in a house by house and block by block manner without the pressure to move as quickly as possible in the way the USAR people must respond.

We had activated the DAE cadres but we knew we needed more people. I am focusing this chapter on New Orleans, but Louisiana was one of several concerns. We had to deal with Florida, Mississippi, and other locations. Each crisis area required more DAEs.

My staff knew that we would be short, so someone sent a memo to Secretary Chertoff. It said something to the effect that we needed a thousand volunteers from within the DHS (Department of Homeland Security), and it was sent with an unauthorized autopen signature of my name.

According to the Associated Press, at 11 a.m. central time, "Brown's memo to Chertoff described Katrina as 'this near catastrophic event' but otherwise lacked any urgent language. The memo politely ended, 'Thank you for your consideration in helping us to meet our responsibilities.'"

I like to think I am not a fool who would send something so silly, both in writing style and as a serious request. The memo stated that the volunteers, critically needed right now, would have to first travel to Atlanta, Georgia, for proper training. That training meant that they would learn how to handle the press and how to treat the public they were to help. They would be reminded that sexual, racial, and ethnic discrimination would not be tolerated, as well as learning how they might inadvertently act inappropriately. They would learn what constituted sexual harassment. In all, if they first went to Atlanta for the training the government insisted upon, it was likely that one or two weeks would pass before they could be considered trained for working in the Gulf Coast regions affected by Katrina.

The memo was transmitted to all 180,000 people in DHS, including Secretary Michael Chertoff. Many of the employees were bemused, outraged, or annoyed, and among them was someone who released it to the press.

I was annoyed because my name was attached and I had known nothing about it. I also found the memo laughable. It was typical government thinking. An emergency exists for several parts of the country. Help is needed at once. One thousand people were to volunteer and prepare to travel. Oh, and by the way, stop off in Atlanta for training that will probably last longer than the time to meet the most critical need.

The memo was naturally quoted in the media after being leaked. I would have published it myself as an example of idiocy in government had I been a member of the press. There was no reason to contact me to check on the accuracy. My name was right there where it should be, and saying someone used an autopen would sound like the cop-out of a liar.

* * *

As to the weather situation that Monday morning, a frustrated Max Mayfield probably put it best: "I also want to make absolutely clear to everyone that the greatest potential for large loss of lives is still in the coastal areas from the storm surge. . . . I don't think anyone can tell you with any confidence right now whether the levees will be topped or not, but there's obviously a very, very grave concern."

The Superdome was damaged by early afternoon as I had predicted and expressed during the videoconferences. And while there were medical teams and supplies in the Superdome in advance of the storm, there was only six days of food available for the ten thousand people inside—if they got lucky. As I have said, FEMA was on-site before the storm landed, but simply did not have enough personnel, equipment, or material to respond. Eight oil refineries were closed and others were damaged. All airports were closed. And the Coast Guard, doing what it does best, rescued twelve hundred people from the initial flooding.

AND THEN IT BECAME SURREAL

The American people were watching as one of the storied cities of the United States was literally blown apart by Hurricane Katrina. Deaths might be in the thousands. Property damage might be in the hundreds of millions of dollars. When the eye of the hurricane made landfall near Buras, Louisiana, at 6:10 a.m. on Monday morning, Katrina was a Category 4 that destroyed nearly every building. Greater New Orleans was without electric power, and the Superdome generators were limited to supplying weak lighting. There would be no air conditioning or other amenities to provide comfort, just the minimum needed for safety and survival.

There was nothing George W. Bush could do to change anything that was happening, and probably most Americans understood this. That did not mean that they wanted the nation's leader to behave as though it was business as usual. Unfortunately, in many ways he did.

The President was constantly being apprised of what was going on in New Orleans, but instead of canceling unrelated speeches and photo opportunities, he seemed to be throwing himself into all manner of inappropriate photo opportunities.

The Louisiana paper, the *Times-Picayune*, carried the news that "a large section of the vital 17th Street Canal levee, where it connects to the brand new 'hurricane proof' Old Hammond Highway Bridge, gave way late Monday morning in Bucktown after Katrina's fiercest winds were well north." The item was mentioned on wire services, television, and radio news networks throughout the country. Then, often in the same broadcasts, was a late morning photo opportunity. First the President flew to Arizona to boost Republican Senator John McCain's image by presenting him with a birthday cake. He also used the visit to a state popular with retirees to announce a new Medicare drug benefit. This same benefit would be discussed a little more than five hours later after he flew to California to talk with seniors and others about the future of both Medicare and Social Security. It was also learned that the President had an important telephone conversation with Michael Chertoff, the head of Homeland Security, though not to discuss Katrina or the devastation and rebuilding of New Orleans—the greatest concern of the moment. Instead, the discussion was reportedly centered solely on the less immediate issue of immigration.

There was one important presidential action that day. The eye of the hurricane had passed over the city, after which President Bush announced an emergency disaster for Louisiana, Mississippi, and Alabama. This was the first formal step in the recovery effort. Everything we did prior to this time was on an emergency basis with no formal declarations. The morning of the 29th, President Bush made the formal declaration of a disaster.

The difference was subtle unless you were suffering. The emergency declaration meant that the affected cities would get whatever support they needed that was within the ability of FEMA to provide. This also meant that instead of just helping fire departments, police departments, search and rescue teams, and other first responders, individual assistance (IA) could be provided. Men and women whose lives had been disrupted, whose possessions had been lost, whose place of employment might have been destroyed, could now count on federal help to restart their lives. This step of major importance to the people who lived in the hurricane-affected cities was diminished by the timing. The latest announcement was meant to assure survivors that resources were open to the average person. Unfortunately, the prompt announcement might have improved the government's image, but it was countered by other actions by the President and several high officials.

I know that many events involving the White House were scheduled before Hurricane Katrina became a danger, much less a reality. I know that the President might have wanted to show that he was on top of all American concerns, not just Katrina. But there were two more events that night, both taking place at 8 p.m. central time, and participation by members of the Bush administration may have seemed callous.

The first event involved Secretary of Defense Donald Rumsfeld whose position ensured he had a vested interest in protecting our country from outside aggressors at a time of natural disaster. He went to Petco Park in San Diego to sit with John Moores, the owner of the San Diego Padres, and watch a baseball game.

As for George W. Bush, he received an urgent call from Governor Blanco who said, in part, "We need everything you've got." The President of the United States went to bed without acting on the request, probably because by that time he had done everything he could within the limited power of his office. All appropriate agencies were engaged, all procedures were known to the leaders involved, including Governor Blanco, so there was little or nothing else he could do. Still, it only fueled the narrative that the administration was insensitive to the disaster.

Sometime later a second levee failed, and by morning water flooded 80 percent of New Orleans. Then the reports started coming in, such as water rising in St. Rita's Nursing Facility in St. Bernard Parish, where thirty-five people died between 8:15 a.m. and 8:45 a.m.

Even the rescuers were endangered. The Waveland police headquarters faced three feet of flooding in fifteen minutes, forcing the twenty-seven people inside to swim desperately to whatever would either help them get to higher ground or stay afloat. The water rose another seven feet over the next two hours before the men and women could be saved.

* * *

On December 14, 2005, Governor Blanco would appear at a hearing on Capitol Hill in Washington, D.C. She would also be the subject of a CBS/AP news story by Sean Alfano. During the hearing the issue of levee failure first became clear, though it would take several more years before all the facts were known. However, on the 14th the governor was quoted as saying of the residents who did not heed the evacuation request, "There are always people who believe they are tougher than storms. And you know what, they were right. If the levee[s] hadn't failed, they wouldn't have been in any trouble and all those people in the dome would have walked home."

The problem was that levees *did* fail, and again in the CBS story, correspondent Gloria Borger had Senator Susan Collins, R-ME, chairman of the Senate Homeland Security and Governmental Affairs Committee, explain one of the possible reasons why. "The only qualification [required for working on the levees] was that you had to be a resident of Louisiana. You didn't have to have an engineer, you didn't have to know anything about levees."

But those were details that would begin revealing the truth. At the time that the first levee failed, the Army Corps of Engineers reported that they believed that a barge had broken loose during the storm, then crashed into the flood wall. It was a nice story and it was repeated by many in the media as the justification for the "unavoidable" increase in flooding in the Lower Ninth Ward.

The flooding was in progress. The storm was still moving through the area. No one had any carefully confirmed explanations for what was happening, but later investigation would reveal that maintenance had been nonexistent or far from adequate for years. By putting out a release that a barge had caused the damage, something that was highly improbable at best and unconfirmed at the moment, the Army Corps of Engineers deflected responsibility. A storm surge strong enough to knock a barge loose from its moorings was certainly strong enough to damage a levee.

Hurricane or not, New Orleans was a popular tourist destination and there were tourists still in many of the hotels as the storm came in. Little thought had been given about what to do with the tourists; the locals were relying on the mayor for guidance, and the mayor delayed giving orders that might have removed them from the city in time. Finally, the hotel personnel decided that since the convention center adjoined some of the hotels, and since locals had already broken into the convention center, they would send their guests there for shelter.

Note that I said they had "broken into the convention center." It was never stocked with food and water. It was never built well enough to survive a major storm. It was never part of anyone's plans including the last-minute locations the mayor was announcing. As a result, we were unaware that the convention center was filling up with people seeking refuge but finding a new form of hell.

The problems with using the Superdome, which would soon have two holes blown through the roof, were magnified by the takeover of the convention center. The news media had been told horror stories about the Superdome when they went inside to report what was happening. One person talked of rapes, another of murder, and yet another of gangs robbing people randomly. Never did the "witness" see the crime directly. It was always a friend who told the person, or something "everyone" knew, or even a seemingly reliable witness such as when a doctor reported a sniper being on a ledge directly overhead. No one else saw the sniper. No one else heard the sniper. There were no bullet holes found in the area the sniper would have hit from the reported angle of gunfire. But the doctor was convinced of the reality.

The convention center was another matter altogether. It was a building that had been forced open. There were meeting rooms and other places where doors could be closed and locked, the people inside unseen and unheard by passersby. There was little to no security. Law enforcement had not been assigned to what should have been an unused structure. Almost all necessities were unavailable to the people trapped inside and it was there that there were legitimate reports of crimes and suffering. What was never explained was that the location should not have been used in the first place.

CHAPTER 8

THE AFTERMATH BEGINS

AUGUST 30, 2005: Hurricane Katrina rode out of New Orleans on a wave of anger, fear, fantasy, rumor, hatemongering, and misinformation. As we had anticipated, 80 percent of the city was under water, houses destroyed or unlivable, businesses lucky to save critical documents and a few pieces of furniture. The Old City, the area where the Indians first learned to settle to avoid being killed by hurricanes, was filled with survivors. Some were drinking in the world-famous French Quarter, the Old City section where restaurants and musicians vied for tourist dollars previously flowing like tap water. By that Tuesday, most were celebrating their survival while numbing themselves to the fear of an unknown future. Others were looting along Canal Street, forcing law enforcement officers to take time away from rescue work to patrol against the thieves, which outraged some of the local officials. Councilwoman Jackie Clarkson was quoted by the Associated Press as saying, "The looting is out of control. The French Quarter has been attacked." Then she added a prescient comment that would hint at a future problem when local law enforcement officers began walking off their jobs. She said, "We're using exhausted, scarce police to control looting when they should be used for search and rescue while we still have people on rooftops."

Optimists with blinders decided that if the French Quarter could sustain life, all was well. More than fifteen hundred people were dead, and the floodwaters were expected to sicken thousands more. But camera crews were drawn to two primary photo opportunities—the Superdome, where people were hot, hungry, thirsty, and increasingly fearful of rumors of rapes, murders, gang wars, and the like, and the French Quarter, where the drunks were living examples of the well-known cry to "let the good times roll." (The Superdome, though a miserable place to be in the midst of heat and humidity, was not having the rumored problems of lawlessness. There was enough security to keep those seeking refuge from abusing one another. By contrast, the convention center was the site of violence of all types, security coming too little and too late since the building had been locked down and was not a planned shelter of last resort by either the mayor or the governor.)

In one of the horrible ironies of the moment, the French Quarter restaurants had been stocked with food before the storm struck New Orleans. The Superdome, a last-minute shelter, had only limited supplies. The two areas were a short drive apart, but the floodwaters made them two widely separated islands. There was no way to move the food from one location to the other before it began to spoil.

Governor Blanco, flying over the destruction in her state before appearing on CNN's *The Situation Room*, commented that there was such deep water in Jefferson Parish that automobiles were submerged and the drivers and passengers had to be rescued. Adding to the problem was the fact that some people being rescued were ones who had tried to return to the area immediately after the storm had passed, but then the levees broke. They had been safe where they rode out Katrina.

My responsibility in all this was not just Louisiana. Biloxi, Mississippi, had the appearance of a war zone where almost all homes were rubble. So many people needed to be rescued that the USAR teams did not bother removing corpses. Instead, each home that held a body was marked with spray paint to alert those who would come later to retrieve the dead.

"We know that there are tens or hundreds of thousands of people in Louisiana that need to be rescued," a Mississippi state government official (never identified when the videoconferencing tape was obtained by the Associated Press) stated during one of our meetings that Monday, "but we would just ask you, we desperately need to get our share of assets because we'll have people dying, not because of water coming up, but because we can't get them medical treatment in our affected counties."

Alabama had the fewest problems; they had roads blocked by downed trees, a half-million power outages throughout the state, and flooding, but it was nowhere near the damage sustained by other states.

U.S. Coast Guard captain Pete Simons explained how they were conducting Louisiana rescue operations as they were the one organization for which this work was routine. Crews were brought to the area from around the country though they concentrated in New Orleans where, Captain Simons said, "we have 22 aircraft, helicopters, that have been conducting rescue operations in the downtown area, plucking people off of rooftops and, depending upon whether or not they require medical attention or just delivery to high ground, taking them to the Superdome or to the nearest available safe spot and then returning for additional people." The Coast Guard was so skilled that they had transported thousands of residents in the previous twenty-four hours.

This was another area of controversy that eventually led to lawsuits (thrown out by the judges) in federal court. We had to keep the greatest number of people safe in the shortest amount of time and this meant creating a triage of care. We did not take them directly from point of rescue to whatever shelter they would be using, a situation that many people did not understand. The media were critical instead of asking why, but our methods were simple, logical, and allowed for maximum rescues.

First we rescued people from rooftops, often by helicopter. Then they were taken to the nearest dry highway not in danger of flooding. They might be hot, tired, hungry, and hurting, but they were physically safe. Then, from the highway they were transported to hospitals or other medical facilities as needed. It might have been less comfortable than being taken directly from the rooftops to the entry of a hospital, but that would have reduced the number of people who could be saved. Always we sought to maximize our resources even at the cost of annoying people who did not understand how many others needed to be rescued and how much danger they might be in.

* * *

Later, when I testified before a congressional investigating committee, I tried to put the reaction I witnessed into context:

It's my belief that had there been a report come out from Marty Bahamonde [one of the few FEMA employees in the Crescent City when Katrina struck. He was in the Superdome along with medical and rescue teams] that said, yes, we've confirmed that a terrorist has blown up the 17th Street Canal levee, then everybody would have jumped all over that and been trying to do everything they could; but because this was a natural disaster, that has become the stepchild within the Department of Homeland Security, and so you now have these two systems operating—one which cares about terrorism, and FEMA and our state and local partners, who are trying to approach everything from all hazards. And so there's this disconnect that exists within the system that we've created because of DHS. All they had to do was to listen to those VTCs and pay attention to these VTCs, and they would have known what was going on. And, in fact, I e-mailed a White House official that evening about how bad it was, identifying that we were going to have environmental problems and housing problems and all those kinds of problems. So it doesn't surprise me that DHS would say, well, we weren't aware. You know, they're off doing things, it's a natural disaster, so we're just going to allow FEMA to do all that. That had become the mentality within the department.

Despite what was known, many people, including President Bush when he began to visit the Gulf states, tended to be skeptical of the reports if they could not see an immediate problem. Senator Mary Landrieu (D-LA), also speaking on CNN, explained the problem best:

We've been on the radio, taking calls as well, and people that have cell phones that are functioning, sometimes they'll say, well, I'm standing here and I don't see any water around me.

Just trust us that when you get up in a helicopter and you can see the breadth and depth of the water and the destruction, whatever people are seeing right around them is only their one little section, but when you get up, as the governor said, most of the roads and highways are impassable, and water is still coming into the city of New Orleans.

The water is up to the rooftops in St. Bernard and Plaquemines. We think there may be only one major way into the city right now and it has to be used for emergency personnel to get food and water and rescue equipment to people who are in desperate need.

While I say they had blinders, when it came to the President, the fault was partially mine. The incident that is most vivid in my memory came when I was riding in the President's car—"the Beast"—while he and I were traveling through the region of California being devastated by wildfires.

I don't care what your politics might be. I don't care what you think of a particular president of the United States. One of the most intimidating experiences you can have is riding with the President in the car designed exclusively for his use.

First there is the power of the Oval Office. I don't mean the power of America's nuclear arsenal, chemical weapons, or anything used in wartime. I mean the fact that the President is CEO of the largest single employer of Americans. The person who has the power to hire and fire, to shift offices, radically change careers, move people in and out of regions of the country, and so many other actions is the President of the United States, or POTUS.

Then there is the Beast. This is more than a car designed for physical security, though it is designed to withstand bombs exploded from any angle. The tires can run flat. The glass cannot be shattered. The interior can be sealed against chemical attack. And the communication equipment incorporated within the vehicle will let the President talk to anyone anywhere in the world.

Riding in the car, if I am going to be honest, was intimidating. I had looked forward to this time to explain to President Bush how many problems we were facing trying to coordinate FEMA and the Department of Homeland Security. The President had appointed Gordon England to be Deputy Secretary of Homeland Security. England was formerly Secretary of the Navy and had been an excellent choice. He met with everyone connected in his new position, listened to all of our concerns about how to integrate what we did, and was comfortable with the fact that FEMA was critical for both external assault and the far more frequent natural disasters. Others involved with DHS were focused on response to outside attack, a situation of great concern following 9/11. However, as the President could see, there were daily crises impacting regions of the country including, at that moment, the wildfires we were passing. Gordon had developed an integrated response to anything that might happen based on what we had provided.

The problem came when Tom Ridge became Director of Homeland Security. He had a trusted staff that might have been quite skilled at running departments, but they had little understanding of natural and external crises. They threw out all our strategic planning and decided to start fresh using organizational skills but without disaster expertise. The result was that Gordon, after determining that the changes would happen even if wrong, transferred back to the Department of Defense. Someone needed to alert the President to the seriousness of the problem and the need for him to use his position to get involved to see if the changes were warranted. I was riding in the Beast; therefore I was that someone.

I tried to explain what was happening, but when I started, he looked at me with the eyes of someone who was both a bit bemused and a little saddened that I had not understood his actions. He informed me, "That's why I appointed Jim Loy" to be deputy secretary, the same position as Gordon.

Jim Loy had formerly headed the Coast Guard. He had worked with concerns that ranged from tragic boating accidents to planning for assault by sea. He understood civilian and military needs, and he was an excellent choice. But Jim Loy would need help if he was going to challenge the changes being made by Tom Ridge, and I felt those changes had to be stopped. Even if Loy agreed after learning the inner workings of the agencies, he would still need someone in a position more powerful than that of Tom Ridge to challenge him. At that moment, in his administration, that man was George Bush, whose words to me, whose body language, whose instantly moving on to a radically different topic all indicated he didn't get it and didn't see the need to get involved.

That's where I failed. I was intimidated by the man known as POTUS traveling with me in the Beast. I did not have the courage to say, "I don't think you understand how the agency is falling apart, sir. I don't think you understand what we are facing far beyond external attack and regional disasters such as you're looking at right now." I didn't have the courage to speak up and say that a critical department was being limited in what it could do solely through mismanagement that was easily changed. And I didn't have the courage to admit that my ideas might be wrong, my advice incorrect, but that the only way President Bush would know that would be if he looked into the problems himself. Instead he dismissed me with the comment about a new appointment and I lacked the courage to challenge his assumption that the matter was resolved.

* * *

Ironically, Senator Landrieu helped introduce me to the two sides of a disaster I will be discussing here—media and politics. The media were reporting what they were encountering without context. Frequently there were stories that were true only on the surface, such as complaints about a Red Cross convoy being denied access to the hardest hit areas. What they did not say, and what some of them did not realize, was that the flooding was so extensive and so much debris was blocking the roads that the area was not safe. They needed an escort capable of handling the dangers, and at the moment the story was reported, that was not possible. The senator's statement on CNN went a long way to stopping some of the criticism by those seeing devastation out of context.

There was also the issue of the politicians seeking special favors. Some had to do with looking like they were leaders. Senator Landrieu was different. She had been with me, the Under Secretary of Homeland Security, Governor Blanco, security personnel, and two pilots inside a Black Hawk helicopter, checking on the most critical devastation.

I was not familiar with the terrain but Senator Landrieu and Governor Blanco were. My job at that moment was to get information from them so I could meet the immediate and compelling future needs they recognized as they viewed the wreckage and received reports from staffers on the ground. I assumed that the pilots of our Black Hawk were being guided to the neediest areas, but I was mistaken.

We started our flight from Baton Rouge, traveling to both the Superdome and into Jefferson Parish where much of the infrastructure was still functional. There was damage to trees, buildings, and vehicles, but it was the routine damage we always found after a Category 2 hurricane. The full force of Katrina had missed this particular parish, and when we went to the town hall, the local officials were mostly present and able to work. Power was on. Plumbing mostly functioned. Streets were more likely than not to be passable. I almost wondered why we were starting our guided tour of the damage in such a location.

This is not to diminish the suffering the people were experiencing there. All hurricane survivors experience their own type of hell. However, I had been to more than 160 disasters as designated by President George W. Bush from the time he appointed me. I still dream of pain-racked faces grieving over the loss of home, business, and family. I have awakened near tears remembering the sight of a dead child's arm sticking up from the rubble, seemingly certain a rescuer would see it, but dying before help could arrive. And such indelibly etched memories were from the so-called minor disasters and low-level hurricanes.

For the previous few years I had set aside my emotions in order to objectively evaluate what a community could handle with its own and its state resources. I had analyzed what they would need from the federal government. And I had worked with governors and mayors to provide whatever support was within my power to bring. I was proud to be doing meaningful work for people in need, and I was simultaneously on emotional overload for the same reason. In fact, before we knew there might be a Hurricane Katrina I had told those in my department that I was planning to return to civilian life. I was going to leave government work after Labor Day.

This was a favor to Andy Card who asked that I stay on the job through Labor Day—one more hurricane season. I had talked about that with Joe Hagin as I passed by the Pentagon on my way to Louisiana by way of Andrews Air Force Base. I said that I really wished I hadn't agreed to stay on because it had become obvious the disaster was going to be unusually bad.

I felt as though I was on a highway with clear visibility but a road surface slick from rain and snow and a distracted driver heading toward me in the opposite lane. At best the driver is at risk of skidding, but his distraction is causing him to lose more and more control. Instead of slowing and making small corrections, he makes exaggerated movements of the steering wheel, hitting the brakes at the wrong time and with the wrong force. And then he is moving sideways, sliding across two lanes, and no matter how carefully you brake, no matter how carefully you steer to create the least destructive crash, you watch as you helplessly slam into the oncoming car. It was never your fault. The only question was how extensive the damage might be.

Katrina was my rapidly approaching traffic accident. I told Joe Hagin I wanted to leave, to not have to be in the middle of a disastrous response to a little-heeded disaster. However, the truth is that the reality of what we faced, not the fear of what I imagined might come, ultimately made leaving impossible. My decision to stay came from an issue of personal morality. I firmly believed and continue to believe that no one who cares will abandon people in a crisis when he or she has the skills, the tools, and the authority to positively affect the victims. That was why I worked until I dropped from exhaustion, napping for an hour or two and then returning to wherever the need was greatest.

As I mentioned, traveling with Governor Blanco and Senator Landrieu was supposed to give me not only an understanding of the disaster but also information about what was needed from the federal government. They knew what their state responders could handle. I was preparing what amounted to a shopping list of equipment and personnel not available in the region.

We flew from Biloxi to Louis Armstrong New Orleans International Airport. I carried a satellite telephone so I could be in touch with anyone necessary to arrange immediate assistance no matter where that person might be.

We then drove from the airport into Jefferson Parish and I was surprised that the governor wanted us to go there before viewing the rest of the Gulf Coast damage. Jefferson Parish was slightly inland, protected, I later learned, by Plaquemines and St. Bernard parishes to the southeast. Katrina struck Jefferson with only a glancing blow, far from the destruction of New Orleans with 80 percent of its land under water. This was a lesser disaster, if such a thing can be said about a force of nature that instantly changes people's lives.

We arrived at the local government building where there was power and other essentials. Governor Blanco excused herself and went into one of the offices, shutting the door behind her. She came out a few minutes later and went into another office, again closing the door. There was no way I was going to tolerate not being able to provide what people needed, nor was I going to be victimized by what seemed to be a politician trying to imply that Washington was somehow irrelevant.

I ignored what seemed to be a snub and spent the time talking to different people handling different aspects of the crisis. I learned not only what was going on in the regions where they were responsible but also what they were hearing from outlying areas. Then I obtained the details about what they needed so as many needs could be met as was realistic.

I was counting on the expertise of the governor and the senator so I could provide the assistance their state personnel and facilities could not. They would tell me what they needed and I would arrange whatever was necessary. That was why we were supposed to be traveling among the parishes that they understood far better than me. Unfortunately, these parishes were also political entities and I was soon to discover that regional politics seemed to influence crisis response on the state level.

Governor Blanco both angered and amused me as she moved from one office to another in a parish with limited problems instead of taking me to those parishes where people were desperate. I was reminded of my Aunt Sis, my father's sister, whose real name we never used. Both women were kind, soft-spoken, with a gentleness that made you enjoy their company, yet they lacked a focus that told you most problems were out of their league.

Jefferson Parish was apparently important for the governor because she spent so much time there that my staff became concerned we would run out of daylight to see the truly damaged regions. I was not being briefed. There was no laundry list of needs. But the governor was spending precious time doing God knew what.

Finally the governor was done, though she never explained what she had been doing. We took off, and this time it was Senator Landrieu who redirected the pilots away from the neediest areas, though I didn't realize how much more time was being wasted until I noticed that we were flying in an ever narrowing pattern that was obviously a search for something. That's when I discovered that we were in a section of summer homes and cottages known to locals as "camps." At that moment I learned that the senator was searching for the Landrieu camp to see if her family had sustained a loss. The idea that this personal detour was being taken in the midst of a crisis was inexcusably outrageous personal behavior.

What I did not know was that while my "guides" were sending the pilots to areas that kept me from seeing the worst areas, a man named Junior Rodriguez was trying to get the attention from the White House he was not getting from the governor.

After Governor Blanco and I came back from our helicopter tour, I specifically said to her, "Now what's your priority?" She wanted to start moving people and this meant acquiring buses to take them to areas providing long-term safety.

I remember turning to my federal coordinating officer (FCO) for Louisiana and telling him that I didn't care what Governor Blanco wanted in the form of transportation for the people. She was the top official. She knew the needs. If she asked for a thousand buses, I wanted him to get them. He could contact the Department of Transportation. He could talk with school systems or go to Greyhound. I didn't care where he went, how he went about it, or what the use of the buses would cost. The need was immediate. The solution had to be immediate. And that should have been all that was necessary to fulfill the governor's request.

There had been a time when nothing more needed to be said and nothing more had to be done other than locating the buses. When FEMA stood alone, the director of FEMA had the authority to do whatever was necessary to help people in crisis. The director worked directly with the President when necessary, and the director took full responsibility for any actions taken. My staff knew, when I held that position, that if obtaining critical supplies during a disaster would prove so expensive there would be flak from Congress, it was my job to take the flak. I was responsible for whatever went wrong, a fact that also ensured that my staff would act quickly and effectively instead of delaying action while trying to anticipate possible criticism.

This time little was different except for the bureaucracy that had absorbed FEMA into the Department of Homeland Security, a logical merger except that the two groups were at odds with one another. DHS was focused on terrorism and external, manmade threats to the nation's security. FEMA was focused on any crisis that endangered the American people, and that meant the predictable problems of tornadoes, earthquakes, hurricanes, forest fires, mudslides, floods, and the like. Instead of the FEMA concept that helped people in crisis, the new arrangement under DHS meant that some of the newer employees had no interest in mere hurricanes and their aftermath. Picking up the pieces of a wrecked city was neither sexy nor would it garner feature stories in national magazines the way chasing down terrorists provided glamour to the lives of the men and women so employed. Their work was important, but the truth was that it would impact far fewer lives most of the time than would the work of the old FEMA.

In any case, I told the FCO responsible for Louisiana that I didn't care what Governor Blanco asked for, he was to contact the Department of Transportation and anywhere else to get those buses. The governor was always the highest authority in a state, more important than that state's senators or representatives. And toward that end a document called a mission assignment was issued.

When we were just FEMA and not part of the Department of Homeland Security, the approach was a simple one. I would authorize the buses and they would be obtained. If I had a question, I would go to the President. No matter what happened, actions were taken quickly. The "bureaucracy" was the director of FEMA, an employee, and the President of the United States.

It was after the creation of the Department of Homeland Security, after Michael Chertoff was appointed, that we began to hear about chain of command. No longer did the President work directly with the FEMA director. Instead the government was becoming like an umbrella corporation with departments and subdepartments and approvals being signed off at different levels. You need a Band-Aid? Your immediate supervisor would take your requisition and then apply to the Department of Small Cuts and Minor Bleeding. At the same time, there would be a request for a payment voucher to the Department of Lesser Emergency Medical Care. Then there would have to be a supply inventory in case another Band-Aid, still unused, would have to be ordered to replace the one that was going to be used for the small cut with minor bleeding. And finally there would be the written permission to apply the Band-Aid to the skin after determining if the wound had been washed (one form), dried with a sterile towel (two forms—one for the towel and the other for the sterilizer's time in service), and applied by a Certified Band-Aidist (one form with attached copy of the Band-Aidist's latest certification).

Okay. DHS was not arranged in so silly a manner. It was worse, but to cover the stupidity of it, we used an important sounding term—matrixed organization. A matrixed organization sounds carefully planned and carefully integrated, like a finely crafted timepiece with every gear perfectly aligned. What it really meant was an expanded bureaucracy where people had different bosses handling all or part of the same concerns, or they had multiple bosses who had to be consulted for action and approval. With a matrixed organization there were so many layers, so many ways directions could go astray; work could be done, with no awareness, or not done, with no accountability. And so I ordered the buses for New Orleans. And I assigned the person I knew had the skills, was familiar with working with the Department of Transportation, and could do the job quickly and effectively. But DHS had become a bureaucratic alchemist's dream where human lives were turned into pieces of paper that documented human suffering instead of alleviating it as micromanaging sorcerers carefully turned gold into dross.

Adding to the nightmare was the fact that a photographer in a helicopter took a now-iconic picture of a large parking area filled with what appear to be school buses. I didn't see the image in time for it to help in locating those buses. The need had passed by the time I would have been able to get in touch with the person who took the picture. Instead, I had no idea where the buses were parked, what school or agency owned them, or anything else about them. No matter where they were, they would have filled the governor's expressed need to some degree and payment would have been preapproved. Except for one problem within the new chain of command—the request paperwork was lost. There were too many layers between need and resolution, and even if we had discovered where the paperwork went astray, by the time I realized that the process had failed, it was too late.

Not that every problem resulted from DHS bureaucracy and changes in disaster handling policy. We also had the experience of Governor Blanco announcing that she had requested forty thousand National Guard troops *immediately,* and the mayor would later quote this figure to show the betrayal of the city by FEMA and Homeland

Security. What nobody said, and what apparently none of the reporters bothered to check, was whether there were forty thousand National Guard troops in the region. There weren't. There was that nasty complication of a war in the Middle East.

* * *

A September 2, 2005, *Boston Globe* article, "Demands of Wars since 9/11 Strain National Guard's Efforts," had the most accurate assessment of what was happening with the availability of National Guard troops:

> "In the four years since 9/11 that we have been at war, equipment has been beaten up, blown up, or simply left behind," said John Goheen of the National Guard Association of the United States. "States have had to borrow equipment and make do with a lot less equipment. We are short literally thousands of Humvees."
>
> Meanwhile, in Louisiana and Mississippi, the states hit hardest by the hurricane, up to 40 percent of their National Guard troops are on active duty in Iraq. As a result, Guard commanders responding to the storm's havoc have been forced to look further afield for military police and other National Guard units and equipment from states as far away as Maryland, stealing precious time from the relief efforts.
>
> Guard commanders, however, insist that their national network of state militias—the only US forces authorized to enforce the law when local authorities are overwhelmed—has more than enough forces to respond to the devastation caused by Katrina, one of the worst natural disasters in US history. Of the estimated 400,000 members of the National Guard, about 175,000 have been called to active duty to support the wars in Iraq and Afghanistan, the commanders said. That leaves plenty of manpower nationwide to respond to the chaos and misery along the Gulf Coast.
>
> "Even though National Guard forces have been heavily engaged in the global war on terrorism, nearly 124,000 troops were available for duty in the 17 states along the storm's projected path," the National Guard Bureau said in a statement. "That averages to 78 percent of those states' total Guard strength. Tens of thousands could be drawn from the rest of the nation."

Indeed, the top officer in charge of military relief efforts said yesterday that as many as 30,000 National Guard troops from across the nation will arrive in Mississippi and Louisiana in the coming days. About 24,000 of those will be on the ground in the Gulf Coast within the next three days, Army Lieutenant General Russel Honoré told reporters yesterday in a telephone interview from the Pentagon. More than 4,000 will get to New Orleans by Sunday to try to bring order to the streets and rescue people still stranded.

* * *

Apart from the transportation fiasco of the new bureaucracy, what I thought had been a complete tour of the damaged parishes omitted one specific area—St. Bernard Parish, where Junior Rodriguez was parish president.

I had never heard of St. Bernard Parish, though I'm certain I noticed it on the map of New Orleans. I was trying to react to needs and facilitate solutions, not get tested on geography. I did not care what parishes were located where unless they needed assistance following Katrina. I also made the mistake of thinking that if a location was in crisis, Governor Blanco would take me there since she had the final say in what help was needed.

The telephone calls I received were insistent. The White House wanted to know what was going on in St. Bernard Parish and what I was going to do about it. Obviously I had to gather my security personnel and ground transportation and leave immediately.

To this day I have no knowledge or understanding of contemporary New Orleans politics. I don't know if Governor Blanco was indifferent to parts of the state, was paying back political enemies, or if there was some other reason for not taking me there on what was supposed to be a thorough tour of the region hit by Katrina. What I do know was that the governor's indifference to the damage in St. Bernard Parish could have impacted on the nation.

Junior Rodriguez was a character out of Louisiana's past. He was a big man with white hair. He walked with a cane, which he wielded to emphasize his talk, and he looked as though, had he been dressed all in white, he could have been the legendary governor Huey Long or someone out of an old Humphrey Bogart movie. He was probably not above cutting side deals for parish business but he was fiercely loyal to the people who elected him and concerned about their needs. He and his staff were essentially trapped on an upper floor in the local municipal building where most power was out, plumbing did not work, and communication was by a single functioning telephone. They did not want to be rescued since the water and wind damage meant there was essentially no place to go. Instead they endured conditions so primitive, the staff would open a window in a private area of the offices, sit with their butts out the window, and relieve themselves into the muck and water lapping at the floor below.

It was disgusting, both to witness how they had to survive and to learn one more important detail—St. Bernard Parish was the location of oil refineries strategically critical to the nation. If the refineries did not work in St. Bernard Parish, the nation was guaranteed a fuel shortage and rapidly rising prices at service station pumps. It was also a major supplier of seafood. The people who lived and worked there might be anonymous, but what they did was important to the nation, yet the governor seemed indifferent to them.

And that's when I realized a truth about a disaster, any disaster where lives have been instantly, radically altered: if pretense was a skin, it could be said that a disaster strips the surface down to the skeletal structure of the human soul.

There are those who labor selflessly for others. There are those who see the sudden barrenness of the land in a shattered community as an opportunity to build a better life for those who remain. And there are those who view the same terrain and are thrilled that they can use it for personal gain, whether that gain comes in the form of money, power, or influence.

The members of USAR and the volunteers who left their jobs to rush to New Orleans, not knowing what they would do, what they could do, or even how the rescue work had to be organized, all were the selfless anonymous. They neither sought nor needed recognition or special favors.

Junior Rodriguez was that colorful character people both love and fear. As we started toward the rooms where he was trying to work, staff members warned us that he was angry. They said he would be cursing in ways politicians normally avoided in public. They said . . .

I walked into a room that looked like a conference area—large table and chairs all around. I had my hand out, a smile on my face, and went directly to the parish president who was holding his cane and glaring at me. There would be no niceties from Junior Rodriguez. The cane moved swiftly through the air, whacking me on the legs. "So you're the son-of-a-bitch that's been ignoring me!" he said, striking me again. "You're the bastard who doesn't give a damn about the people here!" [whack!]

"You're the . . ." The foul language, each time punctuated with a blow to my legs, continued until he paused for breath. That's when I did the only thing I could think to do. "Nice to meet you, Junior," I said. "Can we talk now?"

I don't know what Rodriguez expected from me at that moment but it was not a quiet reaction. Startled, he looked at me for a moment, and then said, "I like you." And with that we began going over the essentials—communication equipment, a helicopter, meals ready to eat, trailer homes, and whatever else would meet the immediate concerns. I explained that it would take me a little time but he would have everything he requested.

We left the St. Bernard Parish offices and were going to our car when a member of my security detail stopped me. There was a man waiting to see me. He claimed to be with the sheriff's department, something my security people immediately checked and confirmed. He explained that I had to meet with the sheriff.

Almost immediately it became clear that the man who wanted us to go with him to the sheriff held Junior Rodriguez, the most powerful elected politician in St. Bernard Parish, in utter disdain. I was supposed to go see the sheriff and learn the truth about what was needed and, apparently, how arrangements were to be made.

Uncomfortable with the summons but trusting my armed security force, we drove down to the waterfront, following the deputy or whatever he was. We followed the deputy down streets; then turned into alleys when a particular street became impassable. We drove on the levees and we drove through muddy water on what appeared to be sidewalks.

It was daylight. The sun was shining. The sky was clear. Yet I had this feeling that at any moment we would be boxed in by cars with drivers who would shoot through our windows, killing us all. It was irrational and yet the circumstances fed on my thinking.

Finally we came to a waterfront area in the heart of the industrial section of St. Bernard Parish. There were barges that had been wrecked by the hurricane, cranes—both broken and still working—and sections for loading and unloading cargo. There was also what looked like a houseboat if you turned a houseboat into what amounted to a hotel ballroom. I thought at first that it might be a floating casino, but it was the home or office or I didn't know what of the man who was the sheriff.

I don't remember the sheriff's name because I was too amazed by what was in front of me to register anyone in the room. Remember that it was only a couple of days after the worst natural disaster in U.S. history, and there before me, in this houseboat in the midst of Gulf water, floodwater, human waste, corpses as yet to be bagged and removed, and sections of wrecked buildings was a beautifully furnished room with a large screen television, what appeared to be a fully stocked bar, and a buffet table filled with seafood delicacies.

"What do you want?" I was asked. I could eat. I could drink. I could sit back and watch sports on the television. The sheriff would give me anything I desired.

"I'm the real power in St. Bernard Parish," the sheriff told me as I ate a couple of the broiled shrimp. "You don't deal with Junior. You deal with me."

And then I fully understood what was taking place. The sheriff may have been an elected official. I have no idea. I did know that Junior Rodriguez, as eccentric as he might be, was the duly elected leader of St. Bernard Parish, the equivalent to a mayor. I felt that the sheriff was trying to size me up as I was sizing him up. I was in some sort of attempted coup d'état and I wasn't going to do that. I had wasted too much time with too many people. I knew what St. Bernard Parish needed from Junior and I was not going to stay with the sheriff. I thanked him for the shrimp and left.

I never did learn the motivations of the sheriff but Junior, as eccentric as he was, cared deeply for the region. He and I also became friends as I guided him through the bureaucracy of Washington, helping him to meet the people who could do the most for his region so that he could serve his people more effectively.

POLITICS, OPPORTUNISM, AND INDIFFERENCE

There were many reasons I knew that my time in New Orleans was going to be my last disaster, at least as a high government official. The immediate danger was over and we were working in ways that revealed the stupidity, greed, aggression, or insensitivity of too many people in too many high-level positions.

My role as Under Secretary of Homeland Security had been clear. I was the man in charge. Good or bad, success or failure, it was on me as it had been during Katrina when we rehearsed with Hurricane Pam, when the real storm occurred and made landfall in Florida, and again in Mississippi, Alabama, and all other Gulf regions except Louisiana where everything started to fall apart.

First there was Karl Rove who has been facetiously mentioned in Britain's *The Guardian* as the man who "masterminded George Bush's transformation from boozing brat to national leader." Whether or not that bit of personal history was accurate, Rove was the adviser to the President who was also placed in charge of the campaign that led to the President's successful election to a second term.

Karl Rove became interested in Louisiana for the very practical reason that it had voted solidly Democratic when Bill Clinton won his two terms, and it had voted for George W. Bush in the election that followed. But Louisiana was a state that had several concerns. The first was that there was a sizable block of people who registered and voted but were not affiliated with either the Democrats or the Republicans. They might be independents. They might be former party members who had been disillusioned. They might be special issue voters.

Ray Nagin had been a Republican who switched to the Democratic Party in 2002. Kathleen Blanco was a Democrat who became the first woman governor of Louisiana. The state was probably going to vote Democrat even though it had helped put Bush in office both terms. Katrina meant a wonderful opportunity to bring Louisiana solidly with the Republicans.

You could see the cold calculations taking place in Washington as well as the attitude politicians had toward the residents. First, the people who had stayed behind, seeking shelter in locations such as the Superdome, had to be moved. They were placed on buses and driven to Houston where the Astrodome had been specially stocked and made secure for transitional living before they could be relocated out into the city where there were mobile homes and possible vacancies in existing apartments. Some people were driven to Atlanta. And in the majority of instances, the people who left Louisiana were black, low income, and voted Democrat.

The above comment sounds cynical, the thinking of a bitter ex-government employee. Tragically, based on my experiences with the heads of city, state, and national government, I think it is quite valid here.

To give you some perspective, Karl Rove was on Air Force One when we met with Governor Blanco and Mayor Nagin to discuss federalizing the disaster. He was present at the meeting when the recommendation to federalize was made, a recommendation he knew would have political ramifications for the governor. This was because several of us had a discussion at the time that President Bush had taken Governor Blanco into a separate meeting area on the aircraft where they were not able to hear what we were saying. It was at that time that the question was raised—I believe by Karl Rove—concerning "how do we federalize Louisiana that has a female, Democratic governor, and not federalize Mississippi and Alabama that have male, Republican governors?"

The other action being proposed was the idea of putting FEMA people with all the congressional delegations; this suggestion led to my cynicism. This had no purpose that would help the people and communities in crisis. They were already getting all the information and assistance they needed. The only reason for showing the delegations with a FEMA representative was for political purposes. From a practical perspective, the greatest benefit would come by letting FEMA handle its mandated work without standing around and participating in a photo op.

Mike Chertoff worked with Karl Rove and others, trying to micromanage search and rescue efforts from afar. This was not his job. He was not present to see what was needed. He hadn't talked with the people in charge. He was shooting from the hip when he was supposed to back off and let me do my job. I don't know if he liked the media attention or just couldn't keep his hands off efforts that were under control. I did know that he was undermining my authority in Louisiana and making me fully aware that I would not be continuing in my job.

Perhaps worse were his public statements and actions. At 9:27 p.m. on Monday, August 29, Chertoff's chief of staff, John F. Wood, obtained a direct report on the levee breaks and "extensive flooding" in New Orleans from Marty Bahamonde, the FEMA official on-site. Then, at approximately 9 a.m. on August 30, approximately eleven hours after Wood's briefing, Chertoff flew from Washington to Atlanta to attend a conference on avian flu, claiming later that he had read reports about the situation in New Orleans. The reports he claimed to have read were in newspaper articles and seemed positive to him. When it became clear that he had received the dire reports from the scene the night before, he never explained why he had not believed them or acted upon them.

The callousness toward those who had lost everything was highlighted by the President's mother in a rather odd and telling comment. The President and his family are not unlike European royalty. They can live privileged lives isolated from the cares and concerns of the public. Like royalty, though, they are expected to go among the people and do good work, especially after leaving office.

Former Presidents George H. W. Bush and Bill Clinton began raising money for the victims of Katrina almost as soon as the hurricane was over. In addition, on September 5, George H. W. and his wife, Barbara, went to Houston to visit the people who were being housed in the Astrodome. Later in the day, Barbara appeared on the National Public Radio program *Marketplace* where she discussed the reaction of people who would soon be moved into longer-term housing in the city and elsewhere. The impression she left, one which embarrassed the White House, was of arrogance and disdain for the little people.

"Almost everyone I've talked to says, 'We're going to move to Houston.' What I'm hearing, which is sort of scary, is they all want to stay in Texas. Everyone is so overwhelmed by the hospitality.

"And so many of the people in the arena here, you know, were underprivileged anyway, so this, this is working very well for them."

The hostile backlash against the former president's wife and current president's mother came from the statement "working very well for them." These were individuals who had lost everything they owned, often had seen people die in the storm, and had been in the midst of violent lawlessness in some instances. In Houston they had adequate food, water, access to medical care, cots on which to sleep, and enough security to finally get some rest.

The elder Bush visit met with greater hostility than it might have had the White House and some cabinet members been more sensitive, and careful about their actions prior to his arrival.

On Tuesday, August 30, one day after Katrina hit, the President's morning agenda included a half-hour speech at the San Diego Naval Air Station on North Island where he commemorated the sixtieth anniversary of V-J Day, the end of World War II. Following this, the White House press secretary, Scott McClellan, told reporters that the President would be heading to his ranch in Crawford in order to finish his vacation before returning to Washington.

I was livid when I heard the President wasn't landing in Louisiana long enough to use what Teddy Roosevelt called the "bully pulpit," assuring the public that he was supporting the evacuation and cleanup. He needed to publicly remind the cabinet to "give Brown what he needs." I specifically recall telling my legislative guy who was helping with the White House, "POTUS can land in Baton Rouge where the EOC [emergency operations center] is located. He doesn't need to land at New Orleans International."

Some people have assumed that I was angry about the President continuing his vacation during a crisis. Crawford was the President's home when he wasn't in Washington and he had all the security and high-tech communication equipment needed to stay informed. Anyone who has endured some of the hot, humid summers in Washington, D.C., understands the desire to be almost anywhere else for a few weeks. Besides, Joe Hagin was almost always at Crawford when the President was. He would answer the telephone and put me through to POTUS immediately. That was why I wasn't upset with where he was spending his vacation. But I was angry about the flyover, looking out the window instead of landing and making a brief appearance to assure the public that he was aware, in charge, and was using me to deliver the relief needed. It would have reasserted my authority in the crisis so that others would allow me to do my job.

What proved personally important on Wednesday, the 31st, was not the crises we were handling, not the President's actions, but a secure video teleconference (secure VTC), run by the White House Situation Room. There was the usual daily briefing, but this was a special arrangement where everyone involved could be open and honest without the discussion being made public. I had been frustrated by the President's lack of understanding about the seriousness of the situation. The secure VTC was my opportunity to express my concerns. Present in the various locations used for the meeting were President Bush, me, Vice President Dick Cheney, Chief of Staff Andy Card, Secretary of Homeland Security Michael Chertoff (my boss), Fran Townsend from the National Security Council, Donald Rumsfeld, and others. This was where, for the first time, I got in Bush's face.

The meeting started out with everybody talking. Bush then told everyone to shut up, that he wanted to listen to me.

I'd had it. I was exhausted. I'd been vilified. And except for the people who were trying to survive in the crisis, I couldn't seem to get across the seriousness of what was taking place and the problems that had been caused by Louisiana officials' delayed action. Adding to the problem was the bureaucratic thinking of men like Chertoff. A disaster is like a war. There is a sudden need for supplies and personnel, and the longer they are delayed, the more lives are likely to be lost.

For the first time I get in his face, telling him how bad it is. We have a disaster within a disaster. We have a hurricane and the problems from it. We have flooding and the problems from it. The state and local governments in Louisiana are not cooperating. I called Nagin a "crack head" for his seeming inability to think effectively. I told him Blanco was out of her league. This is awful, I told him. I need everything. I need everything I can get.

This is on a White House videotape, and when I was done with my tirade I realized that this was a videotape I would likely never see.

I didn't know if the President would understand any of this. He had been effectively sheltered from the reality, in part because of his ignorance of the geography of Louisiana and the fact that New Orleans was essentially an underwater city when it was built, with only the levees as protection. He also seemed to be yielding to the poor judgment of staff aides who insisted upon photo opportunities that overrode common sense. George W. Bush was not alone; politicians from both political parties had staff members who did not seem to understand the difference between acting in the best interest of constituents, expressing concern and supporting what was being done by various government agencies—and trying to look important by getting their pictures in the media.

The videotape, so routinely made for these conferences that I did not think about the camera when I was speaking, was proof of what was taking place. It also exonerated me at a time when the White House felt that I would make an excellent scapegoat, especially when Michael Chertoff was angry with me for bypassing his authority when I thought checking with him wasted too much time. He was also outraged that I didn't stay in Baton Rouge, coordinating all activity from there. I insisted that I had to fly among the cities affected, to see what was being done, what was still needed, and what could only be supplied through White House authorization. He thought I was a loose cannon who didn't respect the chain of command.

That was why I was so pleased that President Bush reestablished the rules I had been working under since I first joined the administration. Organizational charts are fine in theory. There always has to be a chain of command. There certainly needs to be a paper trail to make certain there is no abuse of authority. But in the middle of a disaster, filling out request forms that have to be checked by one person, authorized by another, and then slowly sent from one department to another until the papers reach the top prolongs the crisis. At best, before I was again told to work directly with the White House, ignoring the bureaucracy of my department and those related to it, paperwork was getting lost. At worst, there were delays in search and rescue, feeding and sheltering the desperate, and obtaining safe drinking water. This was no time for anyone in government to be fighting over jurisdiction, power, and status.

Fortunately the President understood; he turned to me and said, "You report directly to me." With those five words he ended the slow, needless chain of command.

After the President spoke, White House chief of staff Andy Card reinforced all this by saying, "Yes, keep us apprised. Work with us. We'll start giving you everything you need." It was a reaffirmation of how we'd always done business, which was important because Chertoff had inserted himself and now I felt like he understood that we are all in the midst of a mess.

* * *

In hindsight the person who best understood what was happening was Philip E. Parr, the federal coordinating officer for Hurricane Katrina. He testified before the House Select Committee to Investigate the Preparation for and Response to Hurricane Katrina on December 14, 2005. He was more experienced than any of us in FEMA when it came to hands-on experience. As he explained,

> I have been involved with response and emergency management for the past 26 plus years. I was sworn in as a member of the New York City Fire Department in 1979 and rose through the ranks to attain the level of Chief Officer in 1999. During my tenure with the FDNY and particularly during my tenure as a Chief Officer I served in many capacities including but not limited to: fire and emergency ground commander, operations, planning for Y2K scenarios, and as a Deputy Director in the NYC Office of Emergency Management. I have played an active role in count-less disasters and crisis situations, to include the 9/11 attack at the WTC [World Trade Center] where I was on scene prior to the towers' collapse.

After providing his credentials, Parr explained what we were facing those first days after Katrina passed through the Gulf states:

> Were we overwhelmed? The simple answer is, Yes. But what needs to be understood is that at any disaster the initial response always feels overwhelmed. I must draw on my experience as a local responder to give you an example on a small scale of what I mean, and then a larger one. The police officer who pulls up to a two car accident with severe injuries while he operates alone waiting for help is overwhelmed. The fire officer who pulls up to a burning structure with people trapped inside is overwhelmed. But the true professional while responding and operating knows that he is constantly sizing up the situation, gaining intelligence,

shifting strategies, modifying plans, and calling for assistance where needed to meet unfulfilled needs whether expected or unexpected.

I would like to refer back to the disaster of 9/11 and its effect on the emergency personnel operating at the WTC. First, it must be remembered that within the 369 square miles of NYC are the resources of a State with a strong central government. There are over 35,000 NYC police officers, about 13,000 firefighters and emergency medical personal, and these numbers only begin to enumerate the assets available to the City. No other city in the country can begin to come close to the responders contained within the City of New York. The response to the attacks on the towers was immediate; the enormity of the task at hand was overwhelming. Then with the collapse of the towers it was chaos.

Emergency services within NYC regrouped almost immediately and restarted operations, but a full coordinated plan took days. The WTC complex was thirteen acres. The landfall of Hurricane Katrina affected four States and covered an area of some 90,000 square miles, an area the size of Great Britain and it affected millions of persons. Effectively Louisiana was hit by two disasters, first a devastating hurricane along with its associated blast damage, *and* second a catastrophic flooding event caused by levee failures. Hurricane Katrina was the most devastating disaster to hit our country. We were all overwhelmed, the City, affected Parishes, the State, and the Federal Government. (http://www.semp.us/publications/biot_reader.php?BiotID=303)

Parr explained the public relations aspect of a disaster, as was becoming evident in those first few days after landfall. He explained, "Emergency Management is more than just coordination. It is about partnership with all entities previously mentioned. Each of us plays a vital part and any one of us who fails in our part fails in that partnership. That failed responsibility must be picked up by one of their partners and that causes delay, confusion and lack of coordination."

Then Parr talked about the failure of elected officials who made outrageous demands and criticized those of us who were desperately trying to work with state and local officials when the hurricane was still an impending danger, not a realized disaster:

For FEMA's part it is my belief we have not done what is needed to get that message across to individuals, locals and States. We've worked to create an image that Uncle Sam will be on your door step with MREs [meals ready to eat], water and ice before the winds subside. We've created an expectation that in a large or no-notice event (such as a terrorist attack or earthquake) we can never hope to meet. As an agency we must help our partners understand their role in the emergency management cycle (as many States and locals do now). To this end I believe we can do much with conditional and competitive grants to State and local governments to achieve this.

Generally, because response is immediate and local, FEMA's primary role in disaster is recovery. With some notable exceptions, what is described at the Federal level as response is in actuality "response support," that is, supplying life saving and life sustaining commodities [such as food, water, ice, generation etc.] with local and State responders performing what we traditionally call response but as an agency we can do better in the response role.

* * *

Beyond the leadership and chain of command issues, George Bush created the first of the image problems that would have proven embarrassing had he and others recognized what was happening. At 5 p.m. eastern time, August 31, the President, back in Washington, gave a speech about Katrina that fell flat with many of his antagonists in the media, including the *New York Times*.

If the President was less than stellar, Secretary of State Condoleezza Rice truly didn't understand both image and reality. Although none of us thought any enemy would take advantage of the situation, the reality is that a nation is most vulnerable when a natural disaster diverts resources and public attention to one area of the country. Confidence in the government is strengthened when the public sees its leaders, especially people like the secretary of state, working through the early days of recovery. Maybe this is nothing more than a photo opportunity. Maybe this is a situation where press aides arrange for the official to appear on radio and television programs. Whatever the case, Condoleezza Rice, former national security advisor during the early years of the George W. Bush administration, had no sense of image during Katrina. Instead of demonstrating concern and awareness of a national priority, she took in a show.

The *New York Post* reported that on that Wednesday night, Secretary of State Rice went to New York on a spree that included the Broadway show *Spamalot!* When the houselights went up, the *New York Post* reported that the secretary of state was recognized. Instead of the usual round of applause for a celebrity attendee as is common in the industry, Rice was booed. In fairness, Condi might have been booed by the audience regardless of the crisis. That is possible, though I doubt it. I believe it was the unfortunate timing of her New York trip that prompted the rudeness in the theater, not the idea that there was an audience hostile to Condi or Republicans in general.

The following day the *New York Post* again reported on the secretary of state, this time because of her tennis game with retired professional Monica Seles and her attendance at the U.S. Open. That was in the morning. By afternoon, while Mayor Nagin went to the news media, she went shopping. Astute broadcasters caught both actions and juxtaposed them for their visuals. First there was Ray Nagin going before the media to declare, "This is a desperate SOS. Right now we are out of resources at the convention center and don't anticipate enough buses. We need buses. Currently the convention center is unsanitary and unsafe and we're running out of supplies."

Then there was the gossip-rich story of Condoleezza Rice stopping at the Ferragamo shoe store on Fifth Avenue where she was identified while buying several thousand dollars in shoes. A fellow shopper who spotted her, aware of the problems in New Orleans, was outraged and began shouting, "How dare you shop for shoes while thousands are dying and homeless."

However . . .

Everything that was said, every criticism that made the national media, was perfectly valid so far as the reporters and their editors could see. Unfortunately there was more to these stories than was reported, and the nature of news cycles is such that even if there had been follow-up articles, they would have been buried on an inside page and given little attention at best.

Condi Rice was and is a friend of mine. I have to say that up front. She is extremely intelligent and received daily written briefings related to concerns throughout the world. These involved everything that could affect national security, and that included natural disasters such as Katrina. The briefings provided her with information not only concerning what was happening but also who was coordinating whatever relief or response was needed. Like everyone else in Washington, a city literally built on swampland, she took time in August for a vacation. During that time she pursued activities that were more casual than her regular routine; however, the supply of cables, briefing documents, and the like never ended. She had to stay abreast of events and she made certain she fulfilled that obligation.

Few members of the media bothered to see what crises I had been handling prior to Katrina. In 2004 it seemed as though the western states had been attacked by a fire-breathing dragon. Forest fires—some natural, most the result of arson or carelessness—covered more than 4,400,000 acres of land. They were consuming large portions of California, Arizona, New Mexico, Nevada, and more. State after state was being overwhelmed. Had the damage been done by an enemy in wartime, it would have been the greatest loss our nation ever endured. More frightening but not widely reported at the time was the suspicion that the fires were being set by members of terrorist organizations.

Day after day and week after week I was traveling to the site of one fire or another. Sometimes I had to expedite supplies and personnel. Sometimes I simply had to be present, to listen to the stories of the young men and women doing their remarkable work and let them know they mattered to the entire country. In addition, the fires attracted members of the news media from all over the world. Even the most isolated wilderness fire, one located where neither civilians nor buildings were at risk, was visually dramatic. Still and video images were exciting to watch on the nightly news. Add to the flames the endangered, beautiful terrain, the helicopters transporting personnel and supplies in turbulent air, the exhausted firefighters, their faces blackened by soot, and you have news footage more engrossing than a feature film.

I was the White House point man. I had access to the President. I had access to the people on the line. I knew what was happening, what was working, and what wasn't. And though exhausted myself, I had to field questions, supply information, and otherwise help the media without letting overly aggressive reporters and photographers endanger themselves in pursuit of the biggest story, the most dramatic visuals.

Condi had known me and worked with me from time to time during the busy days after 9/11 on the Consequence Management Committee and various national security meetings. She had complimented me to Joe Allbaugh as had her deputy, Stephen Hadley. She had seen what I could do in a high-profile disaster. I had the authority. I had access. I had been working on what to do about Katrina when the storm was still an unknown, unnamed danger. She could bring nothing to the table. It was August. She was tired, on vacation, and keeping up with her daily briefings. There was no reason not to go shopping, take in a show, go out to eat, to work out, or whatever she wanted to do.

There is also a D.C. mentality and Condi probably was influenced by that as well. There are so many agencies, so many chains of command, so much isolation that it becomes easy to compartmentalize. I suspect that one other problem Condi had was in looking at trouble spots and thinking, "Oh, that crisis is over there and I am over here, and someone is obviously taking care of it. I'm not needed so I don't have to be involved." Yet for a scared, hurting public, the presence or lack of a presence of a high government official did matter. She would have added nothing to the relief effort if she traveled to New Orleans. She would have brought no benefits to the people. But her failure to understand how the rest of the United States would perceive her enjoyment of activities they might never have enjoyed or, because of their losses, wouldn't be able to for a while hurt the public's perception of her sensitivity toward them.

Unfortunately, since most people didn't know the full details, and most news agencies went with a short take instead of in-depth reporting, Condi took hell.

Still, there were real problems apart from what Condi endured. On Friday the public learned from a *Newsweek* magazine story what we had privately believed all along. President George W. Bush didn't get it. He failed to comprehend the magnitude of the storm, the critical timing for evacuation, and the increase in services and personnel that was needed because so many people had not left New Orleans. He did not understand that New Orleans was a city built several feet below water level, that when the levees started breaking, the total destruction of the lower regions of the city became inevitable.

Having said that, a more objective look indicates a problem I think many in the country shared. Yes, he didn't get it, but what he didn't get was the scope of the crisis and all of us found that scope rather overwhelming. For example, ninety thousand square miles of the United States, an area so vast it is almost impossible to comprehend by comparing it with some other land mass, was under water. We're not talking damage such as you see after a tornado has touched down—the roads intact and drivable when cleared of fallen trees and power lines, homes flattened though with foundations in place, the public able to walk through rubble in search of treasured possessions. We're talking under water. We're talking the chance of drowning if you were foolish enough to try and walk where once there were sidewalks.

The same was true with the number of displaced persons. Other crises might require the evacuation of a few blocks or a few dozen homes destroyed in the path of a tornado. Katrina instantly rendered most of the people in an entire city homeless, at least for the short term.

To George Bush everything was under control. He had me, someone who was experienced in dealing with hurricanes, who was respected by his brother for his work in Florida. Instead of looking at the Katrina damage as a fresh problem that might be different from other natural disasters, his attitude was typical of the man. He would think to himself—"it's a hurricane. FEMA/Brown will take care of it." That was why it took him extra time to realize that this hurricane and its aftermath was a disaster on a far greater scale than anything else that occurred while he was president. There was greater loss of life on 9/11, and a justifiable concern that we were suddenly in a war we did not yet understand, but the damage had been confined to sections of Manhattan and the Pentagon. Katrina affected ninety thousand square miles, more than four thousand times the land mass of Manhattan. No, the President didn't get it at first. Not many people did.

The other side of this was that the President's staff had become fed up with his naiveté the day before. That Thursday evening's newscasts, routinely watched by the staff but ignored by the President, had extensive, graphic, and extremely accurate scenes of the devastation and death. The staff members who were watching immediately recorded the broadcasts and burned them to a DVD they insisted the President watch the next morning as he flew back to the Gulf Coast on Air Force One.

Normally when the President of the United States goes anywhere, there are restrictions concerning how close to his plane other aircraft may fly; his motorcade route is carefully checked for bombs, traffic is rerouted, and so on. This is a disruption, although temporary. To the President's credit, when I flew with him or he met with me during this time, he was very clear that he did not want anything to interrupt the flow of people and supplies. I was explicitly told to keep personnel and relief supplies moving and to ask the Secret Service to allow it. I don't know if they did, but there was no question that the President was concerned.

The glamorous life of the Under Secretary of Homeland Security. Here I am in Montana disembarking from a World War II–era U.S. Forest Service DC-3 during the devastating 2003 wildfire season. Note the duct tape that seems to be holding a window in place to my right. *FEMA*

A better way to fly: With President George W. Bush aboard Air Force One. *White House*

Viewing wildfire devastation with President Bush in 2004. It's not widely known that from the date of my hiring to Hurricane Katrina we had responded to over 160 manmade and natural disasters, including 9/11. *FEMA*

FEMA and the State Department of course joined in the international response to the Indian Ocean earthquake and tsunami in 2004. Here coffins contributed by the Danish Air Force await their grim utility in Thailand. *Photograph by the author*

With my boss, Tom Ridge, Secretary of Homeland Security. *FEMA*

The President and his brother, Governor Jeb Bush, join me in Florida following Hurricane Charley in 2004. Unlike his counterparts in Louisiana, Jeb Bush was decisive and focused in the face of catastrophe. *FEMA*

The other side of the coin: With Louisiana governor Kathleen Blanco during Hurricane Katrina. *FEMA*

New Orleans mayor Ray Nagin waited too long to evacuate his city as Katrina approached, despite my many warnings. *FEMA*

Levees breached: Day two in New Orleans. *FEMA*

An entire neighborhood under water in New Orleans's Ninth Ward. *FEMA*

Day three of Katrina: We had additional supplies moving in and buses taking people out of New Orleans. *FEMA*

"Brownie, you're doing a heck of a job." While a decent man, President George W. Bush was like any other politician when it came to the blame game. *White House*

CHAPTER 9

THE VIOLENCE BEGINS

AUGUST 31, 2005: The looters have come. Their presence was no surprise. Every time a disaster strikes several types of individuals come to cause trouble. Some are bored kids, scared, separated from any authority, with no place to go other than an uncomfortable shelter. They decide it would be fun to go into relatively abandoned parts of the city and vandalize buildings and steal what they can. Others are professionals, street criminals who see a way to make quick money. And still others are gang members taking advantage of the devastation to rob, steal, and often rape, very similar to the problems some were creating in the relatively unprotected convention center.

The looters presented a number of problems for the mayors and governors of the areas hit by Katrina. First, the gang and professional criminal element knew they were protected by the chaos. Victims would not be calling the authorities because wired telephone lines were down and most cell towers were in ruins. Even if they had been able to call 911, and even if someone had been able to answer, there was no one to dispatch. No police officers would be racing through the streets. No criminal investigation unit would be gathering trace evidence and searching for fingerprints. The city was as unsafe as the movie image of an Old West town in desperate need of the heroic Texas Ranger. Except in New Orleans, many of the so-called brave officers were walking off the job. Some were exhausted, with no letup in sight. Some were in shock, overwhelmed by the flooding, the trapped families calling for help from their rooftops, and the corpses neither removed nor buried because the living were the immediate priority. And some thought being a cop in the Big Easy would be a job that was a low stress way to early retirement, never expecting to have to truly get involved with a community in overwhelming crisis.

Leaders like Ray Nagin were faced with the first critical decision they had to make after the issue of voluntary or mandatory evacuation. Did the mayor keep law enforcement officers working with search and rescue, or did the mayor send them to go after the looters? In the case of Ray Nagin, the choice was to send the officers still showing up for work into areas like the French Quarter.

This involved more than just assigning the available officers. Both Mississippi, the hardest hit state, and New Orleans, the hardest hit city, were facing the same problems, and in each case the governors also got involved. However, the attitudes were radically different.

Mississippi governor Haley Barbour took a firm stance against the looters. They were predators and thieves, and if officers had to be sent to quell the violence, search and rescue would take longer and that could mean more suffering and, possibly, more deaths. That was why Barbour announced that anyone caught looting would be shot. It wasn't a threat. It was what he felt was necessary to restore order. Loot in Mississippi and you would take a bullet.

Governor Barbour also noted that some property owners had armed themselves against the looters. He further announced that anyone who shot a looter would not be prosecuted. It was hard nose, clear, and decisive. This was a regional disaster greater than any other experienced in decades in the Gulf area and there was no time for niceties, no tolerance for predators.

Governor Blanco was also concerned about the looting. She, too, spoke out against it, but she spoke as Aunt Sis might have done. She said, in effect, that everyone should work together in the crisis. Looting was wrong. It was stealing from people when they were the most vulnerable and it needed to stop. The good people of New Orleans should immediately begin helping one another until everyone was safe and rebuilding could begin. It was disaster as portrayed on *Sesame Street*.

No "shoot on sight" orders would be given in Louisiana. There would be no amnesty for a citizen who killed a looter going after his or her property. I listened to her announcement and felt that the outlaws had tacit approval to do what they wanted, a situation that sometimes seemed akin to going to a zoo, opening all the cages, and telling the predators they were on the honor system.

At the same time, for reasons not yet revealed in courtroom testimony at this writing, several New Orleans police officers have been indicted on murder charges. They have been accused of shooting people looking to find food and whatever else they needed for immediate survival. They were on the Danzig Bridge when the officers began shooting, and the information I've received indicates that they were neither looters nor should have been mistaken for looters.

Adding to the problem was the essential need to evacuate many of the people who had used the unplanned shelters Ray Nagin had pointed them to. Twenty-six thousand people were crammed in the Superdome and the authorities had locked the doors to prevent more from entering. Methodist Hospital, which held many of the disabled and seriously ill, had been sealed without air conditioning or adequate venting for so long that the internal temperature was 106 degrees.

Rescue operations continued. The Coast Guard had four thousand men and women involved, along with sixty-three small boats, thirty-seven aircraft, and fifteen cutters. And by 7 p.m. Mayor Nagin declared martial law:

"We called for martial law when we realized that the looting was going out of control," Nagin would later explain to Garland Robinette, a veteran newsman working for radio station WWL and arguably the most popular talk show host in New Orleans. "And we redirected all of our police officers back to patrolling the streets. They were dead tired from saving people, but they worked all night because we thought this thing was going to blow wide open last night. And so we redirected all of our resources, and we held it under check."

Much of what the mayor said was accurate, but when I learned about the show, I was pleased that Robinette reminded Nagin that the federal response had been as good as could be expected given that the government could not come in until formally requested to do so.

Nagin didn't argue with that truth. Instead, he expressed the fantasy that everything should have happened in an almost magical manner:

> We authorized $8 billion to go to Iraq. Lickety-quick. After 9/11, we gave the President unprecedented power. Lickety-quick to take care of New York and other places. Now you mean to tell me that a place where most of your oil is coming through, a place that is so unique, when you mention New Orleans anywhere around the world, everybody's eyes light up—you mean to tell me that a place where you probably have thousands of people that have died, and thousands more that are dying every day that we can't figure out a way to authorize the resources that we need? Come on, man. You know, I am not one of those drug addicts. I am thinking very clearly. I don't know whose problem it is. I don't know whether it's the Governor's problem. I don't know whether it's the President's problem, but somebody needs to get their ass on the plane and sit down, the two of them, and figure this out right now. ("New Orleans Mayor Ray Nagin's Desperate Plea for Help," September 5, 2005, *Democracy Now!*)

Yet knowing how we desperately tried to get the mayor to order mandatory evacuation, all I could think about was NIMBI.

* * *

As with our injects during the Hurricane Pam study, each event seemed to either deteriorate or go in directions we had not anticipated, in part because we should not have had to anticipate them. The first was the onslaught of the media and their attitude of privilege in the midst of what was then the greatest natural disaster to befall the United States. The second was the actions of politicians who either wanted to be seen as achieving more for their districts than was warranted given the breadth and depth of the crisis, or felt their actions away from the Gulf Coast would not be noticed.

First, the media . . .

CHAPTER 10

THE MEDIA INTRUDE

IN THE BEGINNING there were the media, entering a story like little children, anxious to see all, hear all, and discuss all. The story is not yet refined. Individual journalists have not yet staked out their personal territory—weeping families with just the clothes on their backs, devastated business owners watching a lifetime of work destroyed by the hurricane, rescue operations, politicians. . . . There will be something for everyone, and if no story seems outstanding, a skilled journalist will find something to win "brownie points" with his or her boss.

And in the end, when the disaster is over, there is often a second carnage known only by those left behind in the wake: a misled public, underresearched events leading to either unfounded praise or unwarranted character assassination, and always politicians and no-name bureaucrats making certain they are part of the winning team.

* * *

Hurricane Katrina was the biggest story of the day, and news crews from throughout the world gathered in the Gulf states to cover it. These were very aggressive, highly competitive men and women, each of whom was trying to impress a boss by bringing new information to the reporting.

Keep in mind that Hurricane Katrina was not just a violent, unwanted visitor to New Orleans. Mississippi was the hardest hit state, experiencing far more damage than Louisiana. Florida had extensive damage, as did Georgia and Alabama. In addition, flooding from the Mississippi River endangered parts of both Ohio and Kentucky. The total destruction was the greatest in U.S. history, exceeding the San Francisco earthquake of 1906, the Great Chicago Fire of 1871, and Hurricane Andrew in 1992. My responsibilities included every area affected—ninety-three thousand square miles along with 819 offshore, manned oil platforms. This is the same land mass as Great Britain.

We had a humanitarian crisis, an energy crisis, and infrastructure damage ultimately estimated to have cost $96 billion.

For some of the best-known print and network journalists, to *not* be in the midst of the nightmare was a career disgrace, a downgrading of respect, a loss of face amid the hierarchy of the network nightly newscasts. Worse, they had a sense of self-importance, of defending the "public's right to know" when what they often mean is the public's right to know their personal bias.

No place was off-limits to the reporters, at least not in their minds. And if they were asked not to drive to one location or another, they were more likely to think the request was a conspiracy to hide something than to recognize the dangers—flooded roads, downed trees and power lines, cars and trucks tossed like a child's abandoned toys.

Worse in some ways was the false hope it gave to the afflicted. A journalist told *their* story, took *their* photographs, showed *their* neighborhood on the nightly news. The field reporter or the anchor back in the studio assured everyone that they cared, that they would follow the story of the aftermath and the people enduring so much by regularly returning and seeing how they were getting along in the ensuing weeks and months.

They did not/do not care, of course. Maybe there is a rare exception, though that is usually someone involved with an intensely personal story. For the most part the same people mouthing the words of support are actually practicing deadly indifference. They shed a tear with the people they interview, but then are on to the next big crisis, the next news challenge. Today's disaster becomes yesterday's old news. The race for ratings at one event has reached the finish line and it is time to look elsewhere.

Everyone in America is aware of the devastation in New Orleans caused by an unprecedented oil spill in 2010. The oil endangered all wildlife- and fishing-based economics in the area. An underwater camera even showed the leaking oil, with the video accessible on the Internet. But something you did not hear is that New Orleans is still far from being rebuilt from the hurricane that came *five years earlier*! And this time the Democrats can't blame the Republicans and the Republicans can't blame the Democrats. No one has done nearly enough to help the residents, members of the media are well aware of this, and yet they mostly ignore it. Katrina, without the visuals of wind and rain pummeling people, buildings, and cars, no longer warrants inclusion on the nightly news. The past is the past, yet no other organization is able to challenge those in power to finish what they allegedly started after the hurricane passed. The media have shown deadly indifference to what many think is a major role—speaking truth to power.

I had no training in handling the media in a crisis. Worse, most of the media professionals working for the various government agencies trying to relocate storm victims also lacked this training. Even the horrific events of the previous year's forest fires were eased by the fact that the U.S. Forest Service and other agencies fighting the blazes had media experts. Most had firefighting experience before entering press relations, and they could effectively convey information about what those on the line were experiencing.

Katrina was different. We were in what amounted to wartime conditions with problems changing by the minute. Ray Nagin's failure to order a timely mandatory evacuation meant the most visual part of the story of the survivors was playing out in the Superdome. [Corpses in the street, rotting and stinking, with few people available to remove them also proved a great visual for the news. The script readers could start their broadcasts with the disclaimer, "Some of what you are about to see may be upsetting and not appropriate for children. Viewer discretion is advised." Then, having covered themselves with the FCC (Federal Communications Commission) regulations, they knew that such notice would keep everyone, especially children, glued to their screens. Some broadcasts were honest. They showed the visuals, knowing they would grab the viewers' attention, but they told the truth: they explained that the rotting corpses had to be temporarily abandoned because there were only so many workers and many people still needed to be rescued. Most either failed to put the story in proper context or implied that we didn't care about the dead.]

You have to keep in mind that the Superdome, so large and seemingly impregnable as it might appear during weekend football games, was twelve feet below water level. Shatter the levees protecting the Superdome from the Gulf waters and everyone in the facility would drown. The tallest person standing on the roof of the structure could still be in danger from the water. Worse, the roof of the structure broke in two places, adding to rescue concerns, the fears of survivors, and reinforcing the fact that it should never have been used in the first place.

Most of the reporters either did not know the real reason so many people were in the Superdome or seemed not to care. Those representing the electronic media needed visual drama and the sounds of people who were hot, tired, and scared provided a dramatic visual for them. They didn't bother to discover that Ray Nagin had been alerted to the problems repeatedly, that he had been urged to order an evacuation that would have ensured that the majority of people being interviewed would have been in Texas or elsewhere, still tired, still scared about the future, but safe and with help available.

Later their bosses might have them revisit New Orleans and other locations hardest hit by the storm, yet even then the full story might not be reported. A lengthy news feature for television can run three minutes, and nothing is better at setting the scene than footage from right after the storm passed. The people stuck in the Superdome would have had their rerun; even though, by the time the reporters returned, they might be getting on with their lives. But that was "tomorrow." The moment they were on the ground in the immediate aftermath, the stories all had to focus on what would be most dramatic for people watching their televisions at home.

Adding to a skewered reality were the images being sent over the Internet by people with cell phone cameras. The focus was almost always on the poor, racial minorities, and those of limited education or who worked in low-paying jobs. And these people were in frightening positions. They had moved into low-lying areas, into established housing that should never have been built, something they had no way of knowing. Many of these people were second- and third-generation residents of New Orleans. They had played around the levees growing up. They had watched the ships come into port. They had grown indifferent to the hurricanes of the past that had been more nuisance than disaster. They had grown indifferent to newspaper articles periodically questioning whether the levee maintenance by the Army Corps of Engineers had been adequate. They had grown indifferent to the reality that the past may have been a time of relative safety and the future a time of potential death. They assumed that they would work hard, raise their children to hopefully have an easier life, grow old, and die, all within a region of the country they loved.

It is important to understand that I never felt that there was a sudden or even a gradual change for the people living in areas like the Lower Ninth Ward. Instead, I believe that the welfare state we've created caused them to become powerless.

I have spoken frequently about the Lower Ninth Ward, where the residents had become accustomed to living in that small area of the city. They were a short walk to the local bus they would use to go to church, a health clinic, or whatever. And always there were, if you excuse my language, bureaucrats "out the wazoo" telling them where to go, what to get, and what to do. They had rarely traveled to other parts of the city, seen other types of housing options, or learned about job possibilities not connected with one government program or another.

Why would a hurricane create a different set of circumstances? They weren't indifferent to danger. They were waiting for one of the bureaucrats who had long dominated their lives to lead them out of danger if the danger was great enough to warrant evacuation. They were waiting for Ray Nagin, the city's mayor and presumably the person they should trust the most, and Nagin failed to do what they had come to expect.

Suddenly the seeming promise of the past was shown to be hollow. The individuals and agencies they had relied upon for continuity had either failed them or were helpless in the disaster. The residents were emotionally shattered, uncertain about the present, terrified of the future, and with little help in place because most of the assistance had been planned around the majority of residents evacuating the city. And truth be told, the members of the media loved it.

I don't mean that journalists are callous in the face of human suffering. Far from it. When I earlier referred to deadly indifference I was referring to the fact that when a story is no longer the lead, their compassion switches to whoever is in the next big story. Still, in the coverage of the moment, the more emotional a journalist becomes, the more he or she will focus on men, women, and children willing to be recorded as they share their misery. After Katrina passed, the images of hot, sweaty, tired, scared, and bored families with children running amok, no one certain what, if any, of their belongings had survived, and no idea what the next few days would bring made for riveting TV viewing. Even cell phone pictures were used on Internet websites, in newspapers, and in magazines, each showing the same type of images.

The problem was that the media were mostly telling the truth, but it was an incomplete truth. They were confronting people who were sweltering in the Superdome, many of whom just wanted someone to listen to them complain.

It is difficult to try and give an example because most likely you have never been through the hell experienced by the people of New Orleans. But problems are always relative. Whatever the roughest times you have ever experienced might be, that is how you define your personal hell. Think about those days when nothing goes right and the stress keeps building. The milk is outdated and you have nothing but cereal in the house. You go out to your car and a tire is flat, or the battery is dead. You race to catch the bus, but you miss it. You take a cab but arrive late to work. Then your computer crashes, and . . . well, you get the idea. Later you return home and hope your spouse is there to hear all about your miserable day. But anyone who had experienced a hurricane like Katrina, a hurricane the people in the Superdome had survived, would say to you, "That was nothing. I remember when I was trapped in the Superdome."

Still, there are similarities. You needed to share your emotions. You needed to talk about your day to somehow process all you had endured and to find someone who would care enough to listen.

Now imagine all those emotions shared by thousands of others crammed in the same space. They can complain to neighbors who have also sought shelter, but no one wants to hear you talk about what they, too, have experienced. Instead, when a news person thrusts a microphone at you, that microphone becomes your accepting friend. That microphone encourages you to unload with every problem you have endured.

It doesn't matter if there are no alternatives. You understand that reality. It doesn't matter if you know efforts are being made to relieve the situation. You understand that as well. But right at that moment, in the midst of the heat and the noise and the uncertainty, you need to vent, and only the news people want to hear it. Only the news people haven't experienced what you're telling them. And they rarely see the necessity of learning how quickly relief will be provided. Emotions shown on camera get far more coverage during a newscast than a government spokesperson trying to inject a calm, reasoned response.

The reporters all knew their role in this accurate yet incomplete reporting. They never misled the public, but in addition to the venting, they were happy to let the residents give voice to rumors, rumors the news people did not cross-check before a broadcast. "I *heard* they're raping teenage girls," one frightened woman might say. "I *heard* they're stealing whatever money and jewelry survivors brought with them." "I *heard* . . ." Never was the alleged victim brought forth to talk. Never were security personnel able to identify any such problems in the Superdome.

The people in the Superdome often sounded like teenagers sitting around a campfire during an overnight camping trip, scaring themselves with ghost stories. I felt the news media could have put the nightmare in perspective. In fact, they could have been a much needed conduit, supplying the people with accurate details they had checked concerning safety, food, evacuation, and so on. The ones I witnessed just wanted a good story to boost their ratings.

Unfortunately, the false rumors about the Superdome had truth to them when applied to the adjacent convention center. New Orleans officials all knew that the convention center was an untrustworthy structure and it had been carefully locked to prevent people from seeking shelter there. Frightened families, gangs looking for trouble, and others had forced open the doors, gone into the convention center, and were creating real havoc, which had been only the fantasies of some people in the adjoining Superdome.

My role in this is something I am not proud of, yet given the same circumstances, the same exhaustion, and the same unremitting stress, I probably would have acted the same way. I felt that I had neither time nor inclination to try and educate the men and women from the media I thought were acting like fools. I was responsible for handling the aftermath of Katrina, and at that moment it meant that I was dealing with the loss of three hundred thousand homes, as many as existed in a medium size city.

The financial situation was even grimmer. Much of the housing was not insured, but the total loss of what had been covered was $40.6 billion. Business property lost $20 billion, a loss that counted only the structures that were either destroyed or unsafe for immediate use. We had yet to figure the loss in income for the people who could not return to work. We had no way of knowing the trickle-down effect on businesses that would lose significant revenue because their customers could no longer afford, or had no reason, to use them. The loss of government property was $20 billion. In addition, the value of insured personal possessions—clothing, television sets, furniture, and the like—was another $7 billion. The total physical damage came to an estimated $96 billion, more than any previous natural or manmade disaster in U.S. history. Later it would be estimated that if all the debris from the destruction was placed on a football field, it would stack 10.5 *miles* into the air.

I had to deal with all of this, though the most important aspect of our work was search and rescue, and it was within those critical areas that I became most frustrated with the media.

The concept of search and rescue is easy to understand. We divided the affected areas into grids. Each grid would be searched by USAR men and women, as well as officers from the Louisiana Department of Fish and Wildlife and other available, trained personnel. Each boat, helicopter, or other rescue vehicle had the minimum number of personnel possible in order to have room for the maximum number of survivors. The rescue workers were also provided with spray paint for marking each house, building, or similar location.

As daylight approached, we would assign each search and rescue team to a particular grid. They knew how to go from structure to structure within that grid, checking each one, removing the people trapped there, then marking it with the spray paint so that no other teams would waste time going back there. In this way we knew that we could account for everyone.

Like everyone else involved with the aftermath, I was hot and tired, exhausted by the unfamiliar extremes of weather and the lack of sleep. I was constantly being pulled from one area to another, and the last thing I wanted to do was answer questions from the media or take reporters on a tour of the destruction.

"Tell me, Mr. Brown, do you think this horrible devastation could have been avoided?" *Sure, don't build a city below water level in the first place.*

"Tell me, Mr. Brown, why wasn't the Superdome better prepared to receive the refugees?" *Because the Superdome was never a safe place. It's twelve feet below water level. It's only being used because the idiot mayor didn't order a mandatory evacuation in time. And they're not "refugees." They're Americans living in New Orleans, or hadn't you noticed?*

"Tell me, Mr. Brown, don't you think you were underqualified to handle so great a disaster?" *Absolutely! Only a highly paid nightly news anchor could have worked a deal with God to save the city.*

Okay. Maybe this is an exaggeration, but not by much, and I truly had no patience for men and women who had all the answers and none of the responsibility.

The problem increased when we had well-known television journalists who wanted to go on the search and rescue missions with us. This was a great photo opportunity and they thought our people would delight in being shown as heroes on the nightly news. The fact that each trip with a reporter and camera operator was a trip during which two stranded people could not be evacuated did not concern them. Some had been to Iraq, embedded with our troops. Some had been to Afghanistan in the same manner. They did not see that being in the midst of search and destroy military operations was radically different from search and rescue. We had teams grabbing people from the roofs of houses surrounded by water into which someone might fall and drown at any moment.

The worst offenders were ironically those I consider the best journalists. Famous names that saw what was happening and were deeply moved by the suffering. At least one started to weep on camera when trying to explain what it was like. He and his cameraman were determined to show how bad things were, along with the rescue effort, by traveling in one of our boats. I said no.

All I could think about was the possibility that while rescue personnel, both the leadership and the field people, were primping for the media, critical medical care would be delayed. There were storm victims with festering sores, with limbs so damaged they might have to be amputated, with medical conditions exacerbated by the trauma of the storm. Some could survive another twenty-four or forty-eight hours without help. Some would begin to deteriorate. Some would die. The biggest difference among the possibilities was the time it took to reach men, women, and children who were clinging to rooftops in many instances. Not only did they desperately need help, they were at risk of slipping into the water. So far as I was concerned, and I was not diplomatic about it, none of our people, from myself on down, needed to be viewed as heroes. We needed to get people to safety.

* * *

In February 2006, when I appeared before Congress's Select Bipartisan Committee to Investigate the Preparation for and Response to Hurricane Katrina, more of the behind-the-scenes reality was revealed:

> Mr. Brown told the Committee that Secretary Chertoff was not involved in the response immediately. Once he became involved however, Mr. Chertoff called frequently regarding "the most minute details of operation." According to Mr. Brown, "the micromanagement was amazing," to the point where Mr. Brown stated that he "couldn't get my job done." He also said that Mr. Chertoff's involvement "exacerbated" problems.
>
> Mr. Brown expressed dismay at the "whole leadership issue," stating that "the problem I had was, I wasn't perceived as the leader down there because I was undermined. Who was the face of Katrina?" He continued: "In Florida, who's in charge of Florida? By God, I'm in charge. Now, in Louisiana and Mississippi, we've got this whole dance going around. Is Chertoff in charge? Is Mr. Brown in charge? The President? Who's in charge here?"

"Well, in my opinion, the President's always in charge, and when it comes to these disasters whatever the cause of the disasters is, the Under Secretary of Homeland Security, the Director of FEMA, he's in charge. But you can't be the leader and you can't do that when you're being undermined and micromanaged."

Mr. Brown told the Committee that he was "specifically constrained by Secretary Chertoff and told to stay in Baton Rouge."

On Wednesday, August 31, as he was on a plane flying back from Biloxi and a meeting with Governor Barbour, "I received a phone call in which I got my rear end chewed out by Michael Chertoff for having been in Mississippi." He said that in that call, "I was instructed not to leave Baton Rouge." He also said: "I knew that this FEMA Director could not operate under those conditions because you can't run a disaster sitting in an office. . . . I can't sit in a stupid office and try to run a disaster that covers 90,000 square miles and run it like a blasted bureaucrat." Mr. Brown stated that this call was the "tipping point because I knew, okay, this is a different game."

The Committee's meeting with Mr. Brown was a valuable addition to the investigative record. His failure to work within the system did not reflect well on Mr. Brown, as the majority views note. But his statements also raise serious questions about the performance of the White House and Secretary Chertoff that should be further examined.

* * *

At least one of the famous journalists who converged on the disaster area managed to rent a privately owned boat not being used by USAR or local search and rescue people. Joined by a cameraman they moved randomly toward the nearest populated area until they were close enough to a house to take the family clinging to it into their boat. The reporter was shown as heroic, the mighty journalist accomplishing what members of the police, fire department, U.S. military, and everyone else had not been able to do (could not do, perhaps?). And of course the family was weeping and grateful, as you or I would also have been. They didn't care about politics or journalism ethics or common sense. They just wanted to be safe.

Once again we were made to look like fools because of the incomplete story. The random removal of one family meant two things to our people. The first was that the unmarked house had to be checked again because USAR knew that they were to assume that if a structure had no mark, someone might be inside. (The reporter either didn't know procedure or did not care.) Whether by the journalist or by USAR, the family would have been saved. That was never an issue. However, by grandstanding without coordination with the professionals, no one in USAR knew which house had been checked. When they went to the house as they routinely went to every residence on the grid, they wasted precious time looking for people who might be trapped since there was no spray paint mark alerting them that the occupants had been removed. In addition, the public perceived us as doing nothing when the Coast Guard alone had saved several thousand people in the two days following Katrina's landfall. We knew what we were doing and we were making certain no one was left behind.

Once again, in hindsight, we should have allowed some of the reporters to go with us, perhaps establishing a pool situation where footage that was shot by one person was shared with others. This is frequently done with a court case where the judge does not want the press jamming inside the courtroom but where there is great regional or national interest in the trial. Making such an allowance would have somewhat slowed our efforts, but it would have satisfied the media and had the extra benefit of publicizing the devastation and the challenges that lay ahead.

Ultimately the federal response would end. Many people would return to New Orleans and hopefully rebuild their lives on higher ground. Many others would simply remain where they were transported, such as Texas, seeking work, finding places to live, sending their children to schools, and joining local religious groups. The more the American people understood the impact of Katrina in the Gulf Coast, the greater the private help was likely to be for people in need. Allowing the media more access, including letting them ride along on rescue operations, would have been valuable in the weeks that followed. Unfortunately, none of our Hurricane Pam injects took the civilian population into consideration in the manner of our real-life experience.

WHITHER THE PRESS GOETH,
SO COMETH THE POLITICIANS

Sometimes I think that if we were to experience Bible stories in contemporary times, one of the plagues Moses would visit upon Pharaoh would be a scourge of politicians accompanied by a swarm of media darlings. Their presence would spread false expectations, misery, and heartbreak throughout the land. Oh, wait, maybe we *are* living in a contemporary version of Biblical times.

I was a presidential appointee under the direct command of the man who, in government speak, was known as POTUS—President of the United States. It did not matter whether the president was a Republican, Democrat, or Independent. POTUS got things done and the director of FEMA was seen as someone who spoke in the name of POTUS during a disaster and its aftermath. But as I said before, the people who decided what was critical were the governors of the states. They knew their internal resources. They understood the physical damage their states had sustained. And they understood both the short-term and long-term needs of their people. Most governors understand their states' strengths and weaknesses, and in times of disaster are willing to accept those weaknesses and take advantage of assistance offered by the federal government and other states.

What I did not realize was that for many politicians one step removed from the disaster, and that included members of the U.S. Senate, a disaster could be a time to win new votes and it didn't make any difference if their actions had any effect on the disaster. All they had to do was look as though they were influencing the positive events of the day and they would have an advantage over any opponent come the next election. It did not matter if what they did was not in the best interest of the people they served so long as it *looked* to be in the people's best interest.

National Public Radio had a 7 a.m. interview with Homeland Security Secretary Michael Chertoff on Thursday, September 1. He claimed that the reports of thousands of people stranded in and around the convention center were just rumors. "Actually, I have not heard a report of thousands of people in the convention center who don't have food and water."

At 2 p.m. that same day Mayor Nagin appeared on CNN stating: "I need reinforcements. I need troops, man. I need five hundred buses, man. This is a national disaster. I've talked directly with the president. I've talked to the head of the Homeland Security. I've talked to everybody under the sun." [Welcome to the real world, Mayor Nagin. Where were you when we tried to get you to listen when there was still time to evacuate?]

I talked with Governor Blanco about her priorities for the people in Louisiana who had been hurt by Katrina, and she stressed medical care. The hospitals and clinics had either been shut down because of a lack of power, water, and other necessities, or outright destroyed.

I met with Governor Barbour about Mississippi, and he stressed that temporary housing was critical. Medical care was not so severe a problem in Mississippi. They had adequate facilities and were receiving the supplies their medical personnel needed.

Florida governor Jeb Bush had experienced the same concerns I was addressing and he actively arranged for the Florida-based Carnival Cruise Line to contact me and offer their services.

A cruise ship is a floating city. Not only can it hold thousands of people in comfort for a prolonged period of time, it has massive kitchens, extensive storage areas for food, places for recreation, and high-powered communication equipment. The civilian-owned Carnival Line offered us whatever we needed to provide decent living quarters for displaced residents with no place to go, as well as for rescue workers and others who needed housing while they did their jobs.

In addition to the privately owned ships from the Carnival Line, I had access to the USNS *Comfort*, a floating hospital with twelve full operating rooms and a thousand beds. There would be other resources if necessary, but these ships seemed ideal.

It all seemed ideal. Instead I opened the gates of hell.

First, the problem: On September 1, 2005, the first buses were arriving at the Houston Astrodome, which, unlike the New Orleans Superdome, had been prepared for emergency living conditions. The state of Texas had agreed to find shelter and care for seventy-five thousand people, and by then the Red Cross was housing seventy-six thousand in their various shelters throughout the region.

New Orleans, as Governor Blanco noted, was in a medical crisis. Doctors from two New Orleans hospitals made clear that they desperately needed medical evacuations. They were running out of food and water, and the contaminated water throughout the city was creating an impending health crisis for everyone remaining. They had enough power to run some life-support equipment, but fuel was low and they would be helpless very soon.

Helicopters were ferrying patients from the hospitals to other states, and six hundred people had been airlifted. However, there were fifteen hundred more patients still awaiting rescue.

At the Superdome thirty thousand people were waiting for transportation that was in progress but could not quickly meet the demand. Another twenty-five thousand people were in the convention center also awaiting evacuation to anywhere else.

No one in the media addressed why the problems existed. The presumption was incompetence on my part and of everyone else responsible for handling this disaster. Only later, when some members of the media found the report from the Hurricane Pam exercise and realized that I had alerted all authorities to what would happen when a hurricane like Katrina struck the Gulf Coast, did the pressure ease off a bit. And only when copies of private meetings with the President and his top personnel revealed that I had vehemently warned of the disaster and spoke of what had to be done did the criticism begin to ease. Unfortunately, that would be later, when the cities were safe and I was no longer on the job. At that moment I was faced with need, fantasy, and egos.

In an odd twist of reality, one that took more than four years to be alleged, I was criticized by former White House officials for my relationship with Jeb Bush relative to the aftermath of Katrina. Secondhand statements were made on national talk shows alleging that Jeb said I didn't do that much for Florida. He was not quoted directly. He did not make the comment. Even if he had, he would have been correct.

Remember that my job was to coordinate response and meet appropriate need within our agency mandate. The states have the first responsibility to respond to the crisis and assess needs that exceed both their resources and the resources available through mutual assistance

arrangements. Only when the response and recovery to a disaster is beyond the ability of the state and local government is FEMA to respond.

Some states, and Florida under Governor Jeb Bush was one of
them, have been dealing with regularly repeating natural disasters for
years. California has its forest fire and mudslide seasons. Every year,
acreage will burn, whether by natural causes, arson, careless users of
campfires, or some combination thereof. Colorado and Arizona also
have such problems. They have trained personnel. They have firefighting equipment and supplies. They can respond quickly and effectively
in ways that other states without experience could not.

Hurricanes seem to come to Florida as often as tourists. Year-
round residents know when to seal their homes and ride out the storm
and when to seal their homes and leave. They understand the risk, can
anticipate the type of damage that might be sustained, and in 2004–
2005 had a governor ready to respond. Because hurricanes strike so
frequently Jeb and presumably other governors of the state know how
to respond and do not need the same federal attention and support as
less experienced officials in other states.

The result was that Jeb's knowledge and experience in disasters,
coupled with the minimal impact Katrina had on Florida, enabled him
to actively assist the other states. He graciously provided guidance and
equipment that made it easier to assist both Louisiana and Mississippi.
There was no reason to put a political spin on the effort.

* * *

September 2, 2005: Race was eventually injected into the disaster. This
was a period when everyone was reacting to what they were witnessing.
No one had any understanding as to why the problems were unfolding
the way they were. There was still the assumption that plans had not
been made; no one yet knew that the mayor had failed to take proper
action at an appropriate time.

President Bush traveled the area and admitted that the government had failed to respond quickly and effectively enough, at the
same time that several thousand National Guardsmen arrived in New
Orleans with food and water. They also had weapons, suddenly important because real violence had started, including armed thugs allegedly shooting at helicopters trying to transport the sick and infirm to

medical centers that were safe. There have been questions about exactly what was happening when gunfire was heard, identified by third parties, but not directly witnessed by reporting authorities and members of the media. Even if facts were sometimes lost, some parts of the most affected areas had degenerated into violence.

I met with Jesse Jackson, members of the U.S. Congressional Black Caucus, and the NAACP, most of whom felt that aid had been too slow in coming. There was the growing belief among some that the delays were the result of bigotry since the residents of those sections of New Orleans most heavily flooded were black. Some seemed to also believe one of the rumors that had made the rounds in the Superdome, that the levees had been deliberately damaged before the hurricane in order to get rid of the residents of the lowest-income areas of the city. Then, the rumors went, with those residents dead or permanently removed, the city would somehow be rebuilt only with quality homes for whites and upscale blacks.

A minor nuisance, though one that made no sense unless it was ego, was Jesse Jackson's frequent attempt to tour the devastation in a military Black Hawk helicopter. These helicopters are expensive to operate and there was no reason why Jesse or anyone else not connected with the rescue and recovery operations had any business using it as a ride along. I made certain that Jesse had the number of my cell phone so I could help him with all legitimate concerns. However, his repeated request for a Black Hawk ride led to my talking cell phone to cell phone with Jesse at seemingly all hours of the night. Everyone else used civilian pilots and aircraft, paying the cost of what came down to satisfying their curiosity or adding a visual perspective for a newscast or news website. Jesse wanted only the military unit.

It did not help that Ray Nagin referred to the city where he was mayor as "Chocolate City." The idea that there was indifference to the suffering of the blacks became a dominant theme of media editorials and "in-depth" reports that made no reference to Nagin's failure to order an early evacuation.

The belief was reinforced on Friday night during "A Concert for America" produced by NBC. Kanye West, one of the featured singers, expressed his belief that racism was a factor in what was and was not happening in the Gulf states. "You know, it's been five days [without aid], because most of the people are black. . . . George Bush doesn't care about black people."

It also did not help that the President tended to act like a well-meaning fraternity boy who wanted everyone to like him. At 10:35 a.m. on Friday morning I met with him in Mobile to start a tour of the Gulf Coast. In one of the now-iconic moments of Hurricane Katrina, he turned to me and said, "Brownie, you're doing a heck of a job." That was at 10:35 a.m. Just short of two hours later, when he was in Biloxi, Mississippi, the President said, "I am satisfied with the response. I am not satisfied with the results." And at 5:01 p.m. George Bush stood at Louis Armstrong International Airport, which had been turned into a medical center early that morning. In comments meant to be humorous but taken as inappropriate by many in the city, he said, "I believe the town where I used to come from Houston, Texas, to enjoy myself—occasionally too much—will be that very same town, that it will be a better place to come to."

What most people do not realize about that "heck of a job" moment is that just minutes before that photo op, the President and I were meeting alone, inside the holding room just outside the area where the press conference was to be held. I had specifically requested that time alone with the "Boss," as we called him among ourselves, so that I could explain to him, in person, how badly things were going. My motivation in having that meeting was to make sure he wasn't blindsided by the awful things he was about to see, and to reinforce my earlier conversation with him during the secure videoconference that most of New Orleans was flooded, that the mayor and governor were ineffectual in their responses, and that I had executed a "mission assignment" to the Department of Defense authorizing them to handle all logistics with respect to the evacuation of the Superdome and convention center, yet I also wasn't receiving the assistance I needed from the Pentagon.

As I began to talk to President Bush in that holding room, Joe Hagin came in and announced that we needed to go ahead and start the press conference, so I wasn't able to finish what I felt was a critical conversation. Thus, when the President, in his usual cheerleading mode, turned to me after being complimented by my friend Governor Riley of Alabama, and publicly pinned his previously private nickname on me along with the "heck of a job" accolade, the video shows me wincing. I had just been telling him how bad things were and what help I needed. Had he been ignoring me? Was he playing to the media? Did he not understand my position and the desperate need all around him?

Later, on Marine One, I was finally able to start describing to him how we needed a full-court press to rebuild the entire Gulf Coast region and that the coordination had been fitful and sporadic because of problems in Governor Blanco's administration and the failure of Mayor Nagin to order an evacuation when we recommended it. This time I realized that he had possibly listened to me but failed to grasp all that was wrong. Since some areas were worse than others, it was only as we went farther in the tour, with the horrors of the storm damage increasingly obvious as we traveled, that the President realized that what I had been trying to tell him was, indeed, true.

There was some easing of tensions for those of us desperately trying to do our jobs because there were new visuals for telling the story. The Houston Astrodome became filled and two more centers were opened in Texas. Congress authorized $10.5 billion just for the immediate rescue and relief efforts, with more money certain to be authorized as the needs could be reviewed. And because landing areas were cleared for commercial air traffic, fifteen airlines sent planes to begin taking somewhere between fifteen and twenty-five thousand victims to San Antonio.

The use of the airlines during Hurricane Katrina is a story of both government-business cooperation and the inanity of the bureaucracy within the Department of Homeland Security. I had touted the use of the airlines to evacuate people from the Superdome and convention center to the New Orleans International Airport. It would be quick and efficient to simply load as many evacuees as possible onto commercial 757 aircraft and move them to safety.

I thought my logic and practicality made sense. The 757 is a narrow-body aircraft, generally configured with one aisle and three seats on each side. I thought this configuration allowed the quickest boarding for people who were tired, shocked, hungry, and frightened.

Naively, I also thought this configuration provided the best security to move large groups of people from the harrowing experience they just had to a safer venue. The bureaucrats at the Transportation Security Administration (TSA), the people who screen you at airports, had a different take. When I asked one of my staffers at the Baton Rouge disaster field office how the use of the airplanes was coming along, I was informed that they were on the phone with TSA discussing how to screen the evacuees. I was livid.

I walked into the conference room to ask what the problem was, and was told by an unknown person on the other end that they were trying to figure out how to screen these poor people before putting them on the airplanes. I began to scream into the speakerphone. I could not have cared less about screening. Yes, I understood that there were convicted criminals in the crowd, that some might even have contraband with them, such as drugs or knives or even guns. But I didn't care. The object was not to start screening and arresting people, but to get them on a plane and moved to safety.

"But we have to screen them," I was told. "The law requires us to screen them before they can board a plane."

The inanity of that comment caused me to lose my cool. "I don't give a —— about your screening. Put them on the plane, post an armed U.S. Army or U.S. Marine soldier at the front, middle, and back of the aisle, and take them to safety."

Decisions were being made in Washington that had no relevance to the needs on the ground. My frustration level at that point was overwhelming, and was just another example of how everywhere I turned I encountered people outside FEMA but inside DHS who just didn't have the experience and culture of "getting things done" in a disaster. To this day, that phone conversation sits vividly in my mind as a reminder of how ineffectual the government can be. The planes eventually arrived and took off with their passengers, but much later than necessary because of a need to "follow the rules."

* * *

September 3, 2005: Government troops were arriving, planes were working, trains and buses were available. The U.S. Coast Guard had rescued ninety-five hundred people. The U.S. Labor Department authorized an emergency grant of $62 million to provide work for approximately ten thousand people who had been dislocated. Yet, though everything was moving as smoothly as possible, the New Orleans Police Department was being decimated from the trauma and its history of corruption. Two officers gave up and committed suicide from the stress. Two hundred others left their jobs. Only thirteen hundred remained, and how many of them would stay was uncertain. The answer came two days later when five hundred men and women—a third of the total police force—could not be located.

I requested Bob Mueller, director of the FBI, to meet with me and Eddie Compass, then chief of police for New Orleans. Our plan was to show Chief Compass how we would bring seasoned officers into New Orleans from other major metropolitan areas. I wanted cops from big cities so that they wouldn't be overwhelmed by the big city problems inherent in New Orleans and exacerbated by the hurricane.

Director Mueller explained the plan to Chief Compass in a tent outside our offices in Baton Rouge. I thought the meeting went very well. The chief was pleased to receive the help and for the chance for his remaining officers to get some much-needed rest. I told the chief we would pay for the overtime his department was accruing, and that we would cover the costs for the other cops being deployed to his city. He was grateful.

Yes, Chief Compass was grateful, but he wanted more. The chief approached me and, in a very matter-of-fact manner, inquired whether I (meaning the federal government—you and me as taxpayers) would fund trips to Las Vegas for his officers who needed some R&R. After all, how can they relax and rest here where they live, in the midst of this mess, he asked? Could I please pay for them to take three- or four-day trips to Vegas to get their R&R outside New Orleans?

In that instant, I understood the corruption and the culture of New Orleans that was feeding into the other stories I was encountering about the Big Easy. "No," I told the chief emphatically, "I absolutely won't do that." It was my last meeting with Chief Compass.

Fortunately volunteers from departments throughout the United States began to come into the area to supplement the locals who remained.

* * *

Texas had become the center for those seeking safety. An estimated 100,000 had rented hotel rooms. Another 120,000 were scattered among ninety-seven shelters that had been established. Still others were staying with relatives or friends.

Meanwhile, in New Orleans conflict between the governor and the President continued. During several of my telephone conferences with the White House I had broached the subject of nationalizing the response to the disaster. If the President chose to, he could waive the Insurrection Act and the Posse Comitatus Act and take over the National Guard, law enforcement, and other emergency response agencies in New Orleans and Louisiana. That was my recommendation to the President when, during a meeting on Air Force One, I again explained the difficulties we were having and the need for federal control (something I was personally opposed to but believed necessary for the greater good in this case).

The President was intrigued with the idea, so Steve Hadley, the White House national security advisor, General Blum of the National Guard, and I retreated to an office on Air Force One and began the discussions with staffers back at the West Wing and in the Department of Justice to prepare the necessary documents. The President, meanwhile, took Governor Blanco to his office on the plane to discuss the matter with her privately.

I was momentarily excited, thinking that now, finally, after several days, the federal government could take control and responsibility and start getting things done without having to work around the intricacies of Louisiana politics and culture.

After the President reconvened the meeting in a conference room aboard Air Force One, I was certain this would be a turning point in our efforts to respond and start the recovery process. And that it was. In a move that surprised me, the President, instead of announcing his decision to federalize the response, acceded to Governor Blanco's request to take twenty-four hours to think about it. I knew it would be the death knell for that option. Governor Blanco's advisers told her of the political ramifications of ceding control of her state to the federal government, and, of course, she refused. I don't blame her, but it was just another frustration in the entire disaster. Eventually, we didn't need to federalize, as Russel Honoré was brought in to coordinate the military response. A Louisianan himself, he was able to bridge the differences between the federal government's military response and the state officials.

* * *

September 4, 2005: There was finally a stated public health emergency in Louisiana; Governor Blanco at last acknowledged that the floodwaters were toxic and additional dangers were imminent as the rotting corpses were just beginning to be removed.

By now Governor Blanco had brought in my friend and former FEMA director under President Clinton, James Lee Witt. James Lee, in one of the moments I most personally appreciated during the entire disaster, attended a meeting in Baton Rouge where I was briefing President Bush and others on our response efforts to date.

In a public briefing you present your case differently than you would in private with the President. I was in that mode of being diplomatic as I sat across the table from President Bush, explaining what was happening, what we were attempting to accomplish, and trying to diplomatically explain the problems we were having with the state of Louisiana. From my vantage point I could see James Lee standing in a doorframe to the conference room. As I was going through my litany of problems, James Lee walked over to my side of the conference table, stood behind me, placed his hands on my shoulders, and looked at President Bush.

"What Mike is trying to say, Mr. President, is that he has been unable to establish a unified command structure between the federal government and the State of Louisiana since the state is so overwhelmed. I am here now to work with him on behalf of the state to establish that unified command so he can do his job."

I was once again thankful that James Lee and I had been friends despite our political differences. He said with credibility what I could not without insulting the state of Louisiana and making matters even worse.

And in the midst of all this came what proved to be a well-intended fiasco.

I didn't know anything about the background of the Carnival Cruise Line. I knew their ships were like small cities. I knew they offered cruises of varying durations. I knew they were based in Miami. And I knew that Jeb Bush thought that if the company was willing, some of the ships could be sent to Mississippi to house both the displaced residents and the rescue personnel. Governor Barbour had been stressing his need for housing and this was the fastest way to provide it.

The Carnival Cruise Line ships were all booked, but the company was willing to cancel as many booked trips as needed to provide us with three vessels for six months' use. Don't misunderstand, you and I as taxpayers would pay for them, but they were willing to inconvenience their customers to help their fellow Americans. They offered the *Carnival Ecstasy*, normally docked in Galveston, Texas, that could hold 2,606 people; the *Carnival Holiday*, the smallest of the three, with room for 1,800 people and normally based in Mobile, Alabama; and the *Carnival Sensation* that routinely sailed from New Orleans. It was a ship the same size as the *Ecstasy*.

The parent company would be responsible for handling the rebooking of the passengers scheduled to take cruises prior to the end of the emergency arrangements. The passengers would also be given a voucher for $100 from the Carnival Line they could spend in the ship's stores when they finally could sail. Then the ships would be sent where they were most needed, Pascagoula, Mississippi, after the U.S. Coast Guard and the Army Corps of Engineers checked to see if the channel leading to a docking area in Pascagoula could hold the boats.

At the same time, the USNS *Comfort* was being sent to New Orleans to provide the medical care requested by Governor Blanco. I had requested the ship from the Department of Defense's Northern Command under whose direction it sailed, and its use in New Orleans had been approved by Admiral Timothy Keating based on my recommendation.

I thought the matter was settled. The two governors had made their requests—housing in the form of the Carnival Line ships to be docked at Pascagoula, Mississippi, and one of the navy's hospital ships to be docked at New Orleans. The majority of the deaths in New Orleans that were not from drowning or being trapped in buildings, were among the elderly and the infirm. Getting them treatment with the least possible stress seemed a possible way to reduce mortality.

I was proud of myself, proud of FEMA, proud of Northcom and Admiral Keating. I was proud of everyone involved in dealing with this aspect of the crisis.

And then came NIMBI.

One of the first people to criticize the cruise ships was Jesse Jackson. He explained that black people would not go on the ships. He said it was a cultural thing, that the ships were reminiscent of the slave ships that brought their ancestors to the United States. Some of the people would fear being sent abroad or killed. Some would feel marginalized. Most of them would be hostile to going on board for what promised to be at least several days and probably much, much longer (the reason arrangements had been made for the next six months).

I wasn't sure how accurate Jesse Jackson's statements might be. I didn't know if this was his fantasy or if it truly was a cultural issue. Certainly there was a fairly recent history of medical experiments with blacks that made clear that racial bias remained in aspects of government work. The Tuskegee experiment deliberately withheld treatment for black males with treatable sexually transmitted diseases so that white medical researchers could track the course of the diseases. More recently, some women with mental retardation were sterilized without their knowledge or consent.

Both horror stories concerning the cavalier treatment of Americans by members of the medical profession were periodically repeated in newspapers and magazines, usually on the anniversary of the discovery. For all I knew, the idea that blacks would fear living on cruise ships had validity. For all I knew, Jesse Jackson was trying to force his beliefs and attitudes on strangers based solely on skin color.

At the same time I had the feeling that Jesse Jackson's presence, statements, and demands all benefited Jesse Jackson. Perhaps he cared. Perhaps he craved attention. Perhaps he wanted to be seen as a leader. His home had not been destroyed. His place of work was not under water. His future was not a frightening unknown.

I believed that people immediately needed clean, safe places to live. The cruise ships more than satisfied the circumstances. The housing should be offered where it was needed most, and if temporarily homeless citizens did not wish to go there, that was their choice. Jesse Jackson was not the person to make that choice when none of us had better alternatives.

The other problem was one of image, not of Jackson but of elected government officials. The average person looking at ships being brought into ports where they could help the Katrina victims would probably not recognize the difference between private ownership and government ownership. They also likely would not have cared. However, to members of Congress trying to show leadership in the time of a crisis, the difference between private and government was critical.

The most outrageous action, in my mind, was that of Mississippi senator Trent Lott, the U.S. Senate's majority leader who needed to consolidate his image as a powerful leader as he faced reelection during a time of change for the GOP.

Senator Lott understood the realities of the aftermath of the hurricane. His Mississippi residence had been destroyed, though he was not homeless. He had other resources including a high income and adequate personal assets to fully recover. He was also from Mississippi, which, though harder hit than Louisiana, experienced no single area of devastation that came near to matching the breadth of destruction of New Orleans.

I consider Senator Lott's actions in an effort to show his leadership to have been classic deadly indifference. The senator cared more about image than about those who needed help. This had nothing to do with being a member of a particular political party. This had to do with injecting politics into a disaster and not considering the full ramifications because they were not in his best interest.

Florida had the same housing problems as Mississippi, but Governor Jeb Bush, the president's brother, sought a different type of housing. He knew that many of Florida's seasonal and year-round residents lived in mobile and modular homes. There was no stigma to being in a Florida trailer park. In fact, for many residents left homeless by the storm, there was something comforting about returning to this type of housing in a community created in a manner that existed in the past. [Jesse Jackson and others talked about a similar social/rebuilding concept for New Orleans. They did not want the trailer parks, but they did speak of taking the land, then building small communities in a number of different areas. It was an idea I could understand, but I was still upset with how New Orleans had long been treated. The city was mostly below water. The levees needed extensive work and regular maintenance. The most sensible approach would be to follow the example of the Indians and stay on high ground, but none of this would be my decision.]

The problem for Senator Lott was not whether the cruise ships were appropriate for housing. He knew they were, though none of us knew whether Jesse Jackson's comments about the social stigma of such ships for blacks were true. What mattered to the senator—to any senator or congressional representative in such a situation—was whether he could show leadership in bringing federal resources to his state.

The cruise ships were privately owned. Worse, they were registered outside the United States and thus the cruise line paid almost no taxes on their income. They would serve the immediate needs of constituents but the leaders of the cruise line would be the only heroes for their efforts to assist the suddenly homeless. Senator Lott would get no credit for bringing them to Pascagoula even if they solved a critical need.

The hospital ship was something different. It was part of the U.S. Navy. It was cool looking when it docked. It had an interior as visually exciting as the most sophisticated hospital. Photographers could record operations in progress and the medical staff helping people start rehabilitation. Helicopters could land on it, adding the drama of air evacuation.

Senator Lott wanted me to bring the USNS *Comfort* to Pascagoula where I believed he simply wanted to have photo opportunities that would enable him to gain more support for his reelection. When he realized that I intended to put the people of an adjoining state ahead of his political career, he was incensed. He immediately contacted Captain T. A. Allingham, M.D., commander of the medical units on board the *Comfort*, and demanded that the ship be turned back to Pascagoula. [Again, note the position of U.S. senators and congressional representatives: they represent their states on a national basis. The person in charge of the state itself, a person far more powerful within the state, is the governor. My job was to work with the governor to meet the needs the governor identified. While I worked with members of Congress during disasters, it was always the governors that I worked most closely with.]

From: Brown, Michael D
To: Blong, Clair; Altshuler, Brooks; Picciano, Joe; Bossert, Thomas; Carwile, William; Wells, Scott; Lokey, William
Sent: Thu Sep 08 17:58:11 2005
Subject: USS Comfort

The determining issue is housing. I need housing in that MS channel. Am willing to use cruise ship if channel will accommodate. Navy assessing that now. If a cruise ship fits, USS Comfort to NO. If not, USS Comfort to MS. Northcom can exercise decision point once we receive confirmation of channel capacity. MDB

The e-mail succinctly defines the needs and response we planned a few days earlier for New Orleans. It was sent to Clair Blong, my trusted Colorado Springs FEMA liaison with Northcom—the U.S. Northern Command established in 2002. Northcom was responsible for homeland security for the continental United States, Alaska, Canada, Mexico, and all surrounding water out to five hundred miles.

Northcom had the USNS *Comfort* as one of its assets. It was the perfect ship to meet the stated needs of New Orleans, and Clair was the person handling the arrangements for me. I no longer remember whether I had requested the *Comfort* or if it had been offered, but it was available, needed, and the perfect ship for a region without any form of hospital care. At the time I wrote the e-mail, it was on its way to the Gulf from Baltimore, I believe.

As the e-mail makes clear, there never was any question about meeting the stated needs of governors Barbour and Blanco. Governor Blanco needed the hospital ship. Governor Barbour needed the housing available on the cruise ships. The only question was which vessels could go where. We knew that New Orleans could handle anything because cruise ships docked there regularly. Pascagula was the unknown.

The U.S. Army Corps of Engineers confirmed that cruise ships could fit in the Pascagoula channel where the housing was needed. But before the ships could reach their designated ports, Trent Lott revealed what I considered his indifference to any reality other than his political ambitions.

I don't remember the exact timing other than it was when the *Comfort* was entering the Gulf of Mexico, and heading toward New Orleans, not Pascagoula. It was late at night. I was in my hotel room, finally able to get a few hours sleep, secure in the knowledge that the two governors would have the assistance they requested. That was when my telephone rang.

Trent Lott was on the line, ordering me to send the *Comfort* to Pascagoula. "What kind of a FEMA director are you?" I remember Lott saying. His voice got louder and louder, and I started pacing back and forth, my voice rising with his. "They need that ship in Pascagoula!"

The senator was yelling at me, as though he could change reality by being forceful. I yelled back, determined to do what was right for the people who needed what the ship would provide. In the back of my mind I hoped nobody in adjoining rooms could hear me, at the same time not really caring. I knew the real reason for Lott's call and it had nothing to do with any need in Mississippi. Governor Barbour was empowered to make that call. Governor Barbour was the man responsible for requesting what was needed in Mississippi and that did not include a medical ship when their hospitals were fully functional. Lott wanted his damned photo opportunity and was indifferent to all else.

I specifically asked Lott if he had spoken to Haley Barbour about this, because Haley and I had reached an agreement—he got the cruise ships, the hospital ship was going to New Orleans. I had an ulterior motive, too. I wanted Lott to remember that Haley Barbour was in charge. Senators might preen and pose and look impressive in Washington, but when it comes to running a state, being governor trumps a mere U.S. senator.

I guess people don't routinely say no to a U.S. senator, because when he had run out of anything else to say, he shouted at me, "WHY DON'T YOU GROW SOME BALLS AND BE A REAL MAN?"

So I did. And I was.

I said goodbye and hung up on the senator without giving him his way.

Trent Lott knew Washington. He knew that there were individuals who would respond to a high government official without thought or challenge. He knew that I was in full charge of the rescue and recovery effort. He knew that I had to act in accordance with the wishes of the governors of the affected states. He also knew that I didn't give a damn about his position, his political ambitions, or his power to reward those who would cater to his whims. And so he called the one man he apparently thought would respond to his tactics—my immediate boss, Michael Chertoff.

Chertoff had not been in the field. He had not seen the devastation, nor had he talked with Governor Blanco and Governor Barbour. But like so many people in Washington, he was not willing to question the powerful, nor was he interested in asking the person in charge—me—what was taking place. Instead he acted unilaterally against everyone's interests except Senator Lott's. He ordered the USNS *Comfort* to Mississippi.

Suddenly we have what is known as a full-scale clusterfuck. Admiral Keating had been following my request. There was the issue of the cruise ships fitting in the channel, but that had been resolved and there was no reason the original requests could not be fulfilled. However, suddenly there was a question of who was in charge in the Mississippi/Louisiana area despite my having been in charge of all past disaster responses, and theoretically still in charge of the Gulf region. What Michael Chertoff had just done, my former boss, Secretary Tom Ridge, who understood the role of a governor and the federal government, would never have done so hastily and stupidly.

A thoroughly confused Admiral Keating, still looking to the person officially in charge—me—contacted me via my Northern Command representative Clair Blong to make certain the change in direction was proper. Certainly it had long been clear that I expected the *Comfort* to go where it was desperately needed, not where political points could be made at the price of human suffering.

From: Blong Clair K GS-15 DHS/FEMA NORAD USNORTHCOM IC
Date: September 8, 2005 4:52:57 PM MDT
To: Bossert, Thomas; Brown, Michael D; Altshuler, Brooks; Picciano, Joe; Carwile, William; Wells, Scott; Lokey, William
Cc: McConnell Bear SES-5 NORAD USNORTHCOM IC
Subject: RE: USS Comfort
Classification: UNCLASSIFIED

FEMA Colleagues:

We were just informed by the NC J-3 Operations, MG Rowe, that Secretary Chertoff has decided to move the USNS Comfort to Pascagoula, MS. Admiral Keating, the Commander of NC, asked for confirmation that this is accurate information. Thanks for your kind help.

Clair

In the end Trent Lott got his way and everyone else involved with the *Comfort* was left in total confusion as noted in the press release below. We had achieved what could have been a classic vaudeville comedy routine in the style of Bud Abbott and Lou Costello's "Who's on First." The trouble was that this was a real crisis with real needs and a clearly defined response that would have been fully effective. Instead, *no* ships went to New Orleans, only to Pascagoula. All because a U.S. senator wanted a photo op.

From the USNS *Comfort* (T-AH 20) Public Affairs Office
LTJG Bashon W. Mann, PAO
Release dated September 27, 2005

The U.S. Navy's Military Sealift Command hospital ship USNS *Comfort* (T-AH 20) is sailing to New Orleans at the request of the Department of Health and Human Services and Louisiana government state officials. The ship, one of the largest trauma facilities in the nation, is preparing to act as an emergency trauma center for New Orleans as its citizens begin to repopulate the crescent city. During this mission, *Comfort* will be under the operational control of Joint Task Force Rita.

"We are looking forward to helping the city of New Orleans get back on its feet and are ready to assist the people in any way we can," said Capt. Thomas Allingham, USN, commanding officer of the ship's Medical Treatment Facility.

Comfort had been operating in the Gulf Coast region for nearly three weeks. The ship was activated in support of FEMA's Hurricane Katrina relief efforts on August 31 and sailed from her Baltimore homeport on September 2. After stopping in Mayport, Fla., to load additional supplies and personnel, *Comfort* and her crew of more than 600 Sailors, civil service mariners and Project HOPE volunteers, arrived in Pascagoula, Miss., on Sept. 9. In 10 days, *Comfort's* medical staff treated 1,452 patients aboard ship and 376 patients ashore at the Comfort Clinic, a temporary medical facility set up at the city's Singing River Mall. On September 20, the ship left Pascagoula in order to evade Hurricane Rita.

The reference below relates to the men and women who had understood the chain of command, the need, and the orders that would take the *Comfort* where it was most needed. Once Lott and Chertoff played their games, we were all left in confusion.

From: Bossert, Thomas
Sent: Thursday, September 08, 2005 4:12 PM
To: Brown, Michael D; Blong Clair K GS-15 DHS/FEMA NORAD US-NORTHCOM IC; Altshuler, Brooks; Picciano, Joe; Carwile, William; Wells, Scott; Lokey, William
Subject: Re: USS Comfort

I will provide report to this group shortly. Am on phone with relevant confused parties.

The other point about this type of indifference is that time during a disaster is conflated. Any delay in action can make the difference between life and death. It doesn't matter if that delay involves minutes, hours, or days. Delays exaggerate time so that minutes become hours, and hours become days. Delays become compounded, often costing people their lives or their livelihood. Any first responder will tell you that is why they rush into buildings without thought for themselves. They know that time matters and rescue is no place for politics.

* * *

One more political game would be played, this one working off the needs, the hopes, and the sorrow of the afflicted. House Speaker Dennis Hastert, along with other members of Congress, decided that they needed to look as though they were in charge of the cleanup and the people working to accomplish it.

The idea was that each congressional representative would be assigned someone from FEMA who would walk around with a notebook and pen. The congressional representative would go into a crisis area with the FEMA employee by his or her side. A resident would come up and explain what problems they were having and the congressional representative would order the FEMA employee to make note of it and take care of it. It did not matter that FEMA was already handling such matters. It did not matter that everything that could be done to address individual needs was taking place. It did not matter that the FEMA employee's time was being wasted by congressional representatives who had no power or influence. If they could look like leaders, they would be leaders, at least in the minds of people who knew no different.

There was another advantage to using the FEMA personnel in ways that were improper. The congressional representatives knew that many, perhaps most, of the requests being made by the residents were being handled by FEMA. Much was in progress, and much would be started shortly, as planned well before the disaster. This was not something the average citizen knew, however. When their requests for food, clothing, shelter, help with finances, and the like were met, residents thought this was accomplished by their representative, a fact that would lead to his or her reelection. When the requests could not be met for any number of valid reasons, the congressional representative could express outrage and blame FEMA.

As to real concern for the people who were suffering and trying to start their new lives, the people who claimed compassion were simply indifferent. A natural disaster was a political bonus that ensured that indifference to meeting real needs could be as deadly as the disaster itself.

From: Brown, Michael D
Sent: Wednesday, September 07, 2005 5:09 PM
To: Hagin, Joseph W
Subject: Legislative Affairs

Joe, just spoke to Tom Bossert regarding the Speaker's call. The delegation asked for a representative in each of their districts. We decided to exceed that request by putting a seasoned FEMA representative in each of the eight most affected parishes. Those are very knowledgeable, senior officials who know the ins-and-outs of the programs. Each of those report to my program representative in the PFO cell. So, in essence, (and please pardon spellings here) Baker, Jindal and Melachon actually have several in their districts, rather than a single one.

If we need additional people in the other members' districts, we can do that, but they will not be of the caliber of the eight we have distributed now. They could act as information facilitators to get the member's requests funneled to HQ or Baton Rouge. I would suggest that the current situation is working best, but will proceed as you think the WH would prefer.

MB

* * *

From: Hagin, Joseph W
Sent: Wednesday, September 07, 2005 5:17 PM
To: Brown, Michael D
Subject: RE: Legislative Affairs

I believe what the Speaker is looking for is a FEMA rep glued to the side of each member's district representative, actually in their office or moving with them around the district. That lower level rep can be a messenger for reaching out to the appropriate "seasoned" FEMA rep.

A congressional representative with a FEMA rep glued to his or her side—that was a good one, but we had the answer to the problem, which I was fairly certain had been relayed on to the White House where the President would do whatever he felt politically expedient. I explained to everyone that we had one FEMA representative in each of the most affected parishes. We had more FEMA people than there were congressional representatives. We explained that the FEMA people were in place overseeing the aid to the public. We had placed even more people in the field, and though they were not each assigned to a congressional representative, we exceeded their requests. FEMA was in every parish, and there were more parishes than congressional districts. In other words, we made heroes out of fools; we did our job without playing a political game.

I was not cut out for this type of gamesmanship, however. I had been involved with increasingly high-profile activities since joining the Bush administration. But I was made the scapegoat for all that went wrong during Katrina. I had high officials misrepresenting who could do what during the preparation for and aftermath of a disaster. Before all the work could be completed, I was forced from my job and the people of New Orleans were assured that with me gone, their elected officials would get results.

Within one year bipartisan and independent investigations into Hurricane Katrina would show that my complaints and frustrations were valid. The various reports that exonerated those who had worked so effectively in such difficult circumstances received little public notice even though many of the reports were posted on the Internet. The mainstream news organizations generally overlooked the story. But what about New Orleans and the people who lost everything in the lower-income neighborhoods? Five years later, prior to the Super Bowl football game between New Orleans and Indianapolis, reporters discussed Katrina and showed the areas still most affected. Just as they had been in the immediate aftermath, most of the people living in these areas were being ignored and forgotten. Indifference continued to rule.

CHAPTER 11

HOW THE MEDIA FUEL INDIFFERENCE

ANY DISCUSSION of a natural disaster and the reaction to it has to include the story of the media that provide what some might consider our "continuing education." It is the media that can offer the breadth and depth of information we need to understand any subject affecting us and the world around us. It is also the media that can define the parameters of the information we receive. The problem comes when we have to choose our source of information without knowing whether we are selecting an outlet that makes our thinking biased, incomplete, or inadequate.

WHO DO YOU TRUST?

Governments, for centuries, have attempted to find a way to communicate with the governed. During the Roman Empire, the most effective medium was the coin. The emperors used the obverse to show who was in charge and, at times, the fact that a favored individual was almost as powerful. Agrippina, mother of Nero, looked at the coins her son authorized to know where she stood in his estimation. When their heads were both on the obverse, her profile secondary to his, it told the Romans that she was, in effect, second in importance. Then Nero changed the coins, having the engravers move his mother's portrait to the reverse. Not only was she losing power, but by being deemed less important, Agrippina knew she might soon be eliminated entirely. Nero's first attempt at murdering his mother soon followed.

The Roman citizens understood such subtle but blatant messages. They learned to look at the latest coins to see whether the empire was at war in some far-flung area. They learned to use coins as crude newspapers whose information was available even to the majority who were illiterate.

The rise of printers and publishers resulted in newspapers of sorts that could be printed and tacked up on walls or mailed to people. One of the reasons Ben Franklin became Philadelphia's postmaster was so that he could mail his *Pennsylvania Gazette* as far and wide as possible while denying postal privileges to any rival.

Independently produced newspapers, often created to express a viewpoint that was counter to prevailing thinking, began to have a significant impact on the nation. The abolitionist press, for example, was a major factor in ending slavery in both the United States and England. It was not a commercial enterprise. Newspapers were not expected to make money. They were vehicles for communicating whatever news the owners wished. As a result, by the end of the nineteenth century, the variety of newspapers that had circulated in the United States ranged from *The Daily Alta*, a California gold rush–era newspaper, to the *Arizona Republican*, whose political bias was obvious in its name.

Newspapers became a critical resource as European immigrants entered the United States. They tended to settle in similar areas so they could share the food, the customs, and the language of their native lands while assimilating into the new culture. Hence, newspapers were being written in the native languages of the immigrant neighborhoods. The desire for special-interest news went beyond the development of different language newspapers. For example, it has been estimated that at any given moment there are approximately fifty wars taking place around the world—civil wars, wars by proxy, cyber wars, conventional wars, and the like. These might be active conflicts involving several nations, such as the United States is experiencing in Afghanistan, or simmering conflagrations that periodically erupt, such as occur among any number of countries in the Middle East. Our newspapers and radio and television stations routinely apprise us of what is happening in probably no more than a dozen such wars. African nations without desired resources (e.g., no oil reserves, no precious gems, no metals needed for industry) may be controlled by military leaders who engage in genocide, but it is doubtful you will learn of this. It is only when newspapers written for migrants from the affected countries cover these stories for their readers that the stories are disseminated in the United States.

Likewise after the 2010 earthquakes, volcanic eruptions, and such manmade catastrophes as the oil spill off New Orleans, some researchers noted that on any given day eight events we would consider disasters take place in different parts of the world. Journalists pick among them based on the medium they represent and the perceived concerns of their readers/viewers/listeners. This means that headline news in one community is unknown in another except through a special-interest publication such as a foreign-language paper serving an immigrant neighborhood. We thus can become indifferent to human need and suffering because the media assume we have little or no interest in the subject. And though the Internet has greatly expanded our access to information throughout the world, we have to know a story exists in order to search for it on the web.

WHEN NEWSPAPERS DOMINATED INFORMATION RESOURCES

Throughout the last century there was a cycle to the presentation of news. Larger city newspapers, for example, always ran several editions throughout the day. There was the basic material that would be unchanging—advertisements, columns, comic strips, puzzles, articles that were complete, such as a story about a criminal trial that had ended or an interview with a prominent citizen. Then there would be the breaking news such as a plane crash, a sporting event completed during the day, a major fire, and, in what was usually the last edition, the closing stock market prices.

The first newspaper would be on the streets early in the morning when people were going to work. The last newspaper would be at the end of the day, following the close of the stock market, when people were going home. In between there might be one, two, or more editions, depending upon the importance of breaking news, though the only changes would be the necessary updating, and that would be done in the same space previously occupied by now outdated news. Often each edition would have a star at the top so someone could tell at a glance whether this was a three- or four-star edition, or whatever.

A second cycle would involve the first edition of Monday's paper. Politicians learned to have press conferences, primarily with newspaper reporters, on Sunday afternoons. They chose topics that were important, but not so important as to warrant front-page space during most of the week. It was only on Monday, when there was little fresh news for the first edition, that a politician could be assured of meaningful space.

The news cycle would also be determined by the number of regularly planned editions. A morning paper might go to press some time after midnight. An updated edition would come out midday, and a final edition would be out in time for the commute home from work. Business leaders and politicians learned to plan news releases around the deadlines for each edition of their local dailies.

Reporters were faced with limited pressure. There would be those men and women who covered breaking news throughout the day. There would be beat reporters who covered one segment of the news—fashion, or business, or crime, for example. And there would be specialized assignments when a reporter or team of reporters would investigate a news story over the course of a week or more. Sometimes the story would be released as a feature on Sunday. What would have been given space for no more than 1,200 words during the week might be given space for a 10,000-word feature on Sunday. And the biggest stories of a seven days a week paper might be given six days—the 10,000 word Sunday segment and then smaller stories adding information from Monday through Friday.

Before television became readily available to the public, a news/feature hybrid was long in use in movie theaters. This was the newsreel that delivered visual stories that ranged from Hitler's speeches and the increasing militancy preceding World War II to the marriage of Princess Elizabeth and Prince Philip. Sometimes the topics chosen seemed a cross between a popular culture publication and a news magazine, though presented as moving picture stories. At other times they included travelogues with segments introducing the public to distant lands, exotic animals, and strange cultures. Going to the movies meant exposure to a broad range of information not otherwise available. Radio news developed both five-minute hourly updates—essentially headlines read by the on-air broadcaster—and occasionally longer segments.

Science is another area where limited information is provided. Not only do few colleges and universities train journalism students to be science writers, but when science is covered most of the writing is related to major breakthroughs and shocking disasters. The day-to-day concerns scientists face in either trying to understand such phenomena as natural disasters, genetic diseases, and even the challenge of outer space travel, are rarely covered. And when a supposed breakthrough occurs in an area such as medicine, writers are rarely trained to explain the details, the possible risks, and the possible failings.

In the case of a tropical storm gradually becoming a hurricane, most reporters are unable to explain the impending dangers and the ways in which what seems like a distant heavy rainfall can build to a destructive force capable of leveling a city. There are no meaningful images for a medium that requires visual drama. Reporters work with little understanding and the experts are not used to trying to educate the public in the arcane problems of wind currents, barometric pressure changes, and the like. And since the eventual size of the storm and the exact location of its landfall are not known, the information the public needs to decide what actions they will take is given only a few seconds of airtime or a couple of paragraphs in the newspaper. None of this screams "Important Information You Need to Know Right Now," and even those responsible for protecting the citizens, individuals such as Mayor Ray Nagin, cannot be certain what they should do.

JOURNALIST ISOLATION

Anyone who has ever watched a White House press briefing, either conducted by the President or the White House press secretary, has seen members of the White House press corps trying to get attention. They shout out questions. They wave. And when someone is called upon, he or she is momentarily the sole focus of the cameras recording the event.

White House press conferences are never open ended. There is a specific starting time, beginning with announcements the President wants the public to hear, and there is a specific stopping time after which no further questions are taken, no further answers provided. And because the White House press corps is relatively unchanging, the President and the press secretary know who will ask questions that will reinforce the day's message, who will ask innocuous questions that can be answered without conflict, and who will use a pugnacious attitude to get a reaction from the speaker. The latter may be deliberately hostile or ask questions completely unrelated to national affairs. What matters to the questioner is face time.

Over the years, several things have happened. First, the White House press corps has been kept relatively isolated. They may travel with the President. They may provide exclusive coverage of the regular briefings from the White House. They may have the ego-boosting title of "our White House correspondent." But they rarely break new ground or are in a position to do serious investigative reporting. The Watergate scandal that eventually forced the resignation of President Richard Nixon was revealed by two reporters for the *Washington Post,* not that paper's reporter in the White House press corps. All the reporters, in and out of the White House press corps, were competent professionals, but only the outsiders had the freedom to pursue a possible scandal.

Access is another reason reporters dealing with government officials, as well as the heads of major businesses important to a community, are not likely to pursue important but negative stories. Members of the media love to advertise that they will be featuring an exclusive interview with the CEO of the largest employer in a region, or the President's personal assistant. Sometimes the interviews are meaningful, the questions incisive about issues of real concern to the public. The subject is not permitted to avoid answering, and a less than effective response is both obvious and often harmful.

The problem is that usually the first such interview by a journalist is also the last time he or she will be given time with the official. This was certainly the case with Sarah Palin when she was interviewed in September 2008 by Katie Couric of CBS News after being chosen as running mate for Republican presidential candidate John McCain.

Governor Palin was ill prepared for the interview and came across as having far less intellectual ability than the job required. The governor became a joke because she agreed to speak with a reporter the public saw as unbiased and objective, whether or not that perception was a valid one. Sarah Palin later resigned as governor but should she ever decide to run for office again, it is certain that Katie Couric will never again be given an exclusive interview. In addition, all CBS correspondents may find that they are unwelcome in a Palin administration.

Access is not politically one-sided. The Obama administration has faced criticism for denying access to Fox News reporters for their perceived bias. And President Ronald Reagan is remembered by the media as being a man who wanted the United States to adopt a law similar to one in Britain that, under the right circumstances, protects politicians from having embarrassing information made public.

So how does this situation lead to deadly indifference? A reporter who wants to advance through access to newsmakers has to consider his or her best interests, just like politicians. It is not in the reporter's best interest to do a penetrating interview that reveals the failings, inadequacies, or inappropriate acts of a subject if he or she wishes to secure a later interview. Certainly there are those politicians whose integrity is such that they will endure hostility because they acknowledge they deserve it.

In recent years the late Senator Ted Kennedy's image was protected from tabloid exposure for womanizing, excessive drinking, and other failings. According to some of the reporting staff, the senator made a deal with one of the best-known supermarket tabloids: someone connected with his staff would provide periodic stories that were titillating but not career threatening. In exchange, the tabloid would not publish the occasional article revealing a scandal so serious he might have been voted out of office.

In government how you are treated is all about access.

WHEN REALITY LEADS TO ACCESS DENIAL

There is another area of denied access that is rarely discussed or even considered by the media and by the newsmakers whose actions are being reported. This was one we encountered during the immediate aftermath of Hurricane Katrina.

Size matters. A disaster involving a single building—a nighttime fire in an eight-unit apartment building, for example—makes for the perfect media story.

First there is the big picture—the building with flames coming from some windows, smoke from others, firefighters working to put out the blaze, firefighters racing through the building to save lives, and residents clad in night clothes huddled outside, watching the effort to quell the conflagration. This is the scene guaranteed to make the news.

Next the reporters and photographers focus on visual vignettes that tell smaller pieces of the story. There might be a firefighter holding a baby who was just saved—everyone cheering—or who died of smoke inhalation—tears on the faces of the firefighter, the family, and the neighbors. There might be a rescue of a dog or cat. There might be ambulances loading victims inside for the race to a burn center. And when the fire is out, there will be footage of arson investigators searching through the rubble, looking for the flashpoint, trying to see if the fire was accidental or deliberately set.

A day or two later there may be follow-up stories, such as the report on the cause of the fire, the story of any people who were hurt or killed, and perhaps the story of the hero who pounded on the doors and windows after seeing the building ablaze. Each adds a piece to what happened. More important, all the facts are readily checked before the segments are aired and the articles written. Doctors from the burn unit will be contacted to explain what happened to the victims and what is being done to help with their recovery. The arson investigator will be contacted to explain the way the fire was started and spread, if deliberate, and if the fire was an accident, the fire department spokesperson will discuss how to keep your home safe from similar accidents. The number of people involved in the incident is small enough that the members of the media have rapid and complete access, ensuring that they will properly do their job in covering the tragedy.

A natural disaster is an entirely different matter. The scope of the disaster, the number of different organizations involved with search,

rescue, evacuation, recovery, law enforcement, housing, food preparation and distribution, and the like make thorough coverage impossible.
Each reporter or small team of reporters essentially stakes out an area
of the disaster, and then looks for the stories in that area.

In the case of Hurricane Katrina, reporters who were talking with
residents in areas like the French Quarter found that concerns about
massive destruction and a lack of basic supplies for daily survival were
exaggerated. It was party time for the locals and those visitors who had
found their way to the bars and clubs, many of which had stayed open
through the wind and driving rain.

Other reporters, often for the same news organization, were in the
midst of dead bodies, suddenly homeless and terrified families in need
of evacuation, and water that was likely contaminated. People were
hungry, hot, tired, and inaccurately blaming FEMA for not getting
them out of the city before the hurricane struck. And in many sections
of the city, corpses were floating in the water because rescuing the
trapped and injured required all available manpower. The dead would
have to wait.

You could assemble the various news shows and see how the isolation played out. Reporters in Florida praised FEMA and Governor Jeb
Bush for being on top of the storm, keeping people safe, having emergency housing, and otherwise handling the aftermath in an effective
way. They had no way to compare that situation with the one in Louisiana where similar planning had been in place, similar information
had been provided, but Governor Blanco let the reticent Mayor Nagin
make initial decisions concerning evacuation. However, the news an-
chors, even more isolated from the events of the day than the reporters,
assumed that the problems were caused by failures of FEMA personnel
instead of politicians' indifference.

The news personnel who were covering George Bush dutifully reported whatever he had to say, without knowing if he was fully aware of
the damage to the multistate region. Worse, should what they reported
be contradicted by other news teams working in different sections of
the impacted area, the implication could easily be that those of us in the
field had misled the President.

BEHIND THE SCENES

From: Earman, Margie

To: Buikema, Edward; Lowder, Michael; Hepler, Megs; Skarosi, David; Beall, Jack

Sent: Thu Sep 08 13:35:51 2005

Subject: Fox News is reporting that a Dr. Albert Barracos, Methodist Hospital (?) says about 12 patients died because FEMA confiscated three trucks of fuel.

From: Lowder, Michael

Sent: Thursday, September 08, 2005 1:40 PM

To: Tony.Robinson; William.Lokey; Scott.Wells; Monette, Ted

Subject: Fw: Fox News is reporting

Just as an FYI . . .

From: Altshuler, Brooks

Sent: Thursday, September 08, 2005 2:02 PM

To: Lokey, William; Lowder, Michael; Tony.Robinson; William.Lokey; Scott. Wells; Monette, Ted; Brown, Michael D; Bahamonde, Marty; Trissell, David

Cc: Picciano, Joe; Rhode, Patrick

Subject: RE: Fox News is reporting

WE NEED COME OUT WITH A STRONG PUBLIC MESSAGE ON THIS NOW. Can we get a public service announcement running along the lines of a recording of Brown for radio and anything else saying that FEMA DOES NOT HAVE THE LEGAL AUTHORITY TO SEIZE PRIVATE PROPERTY FOR ANY REASON. IF YOU ARE APPROACHED BY ANYONE CLAIMING THEY ARE FROM FEMA OR ARE SEIZING PROPERTY ON BEHALF OF FEMA, PLEASE NOTIFY YOUR LOCAL LAW ENFORCEMENT AUTHORI-TIES. —we should also think of an 800 number to call to report.

Trissell—can you confirm the statement—that we don't have legal authority. Arty—can you work the public message part?

We need to get this out soon as the rumor mill is killing us.

From: Lokey, William
Sent: Thursday, September 08, 2005 1:48 PM
To: Lowder, Michael; Tony.Robinson; William.Lokey; Scott.Wells; Monette,
Ted; Brown, Michael D
Cc: Picciano, Joe; Altshuler, Brooks; Rhode, Patrick
Subject: RE: Fox News is reporting

We have turned the "FEMA confiscated the trailers" over to the FBI. I am doing the same thing here. We got to get Fed Law Enforcement investigation
going ASAP as well as trying to do PR damage control.

There is no room for perspective in a massive disaster. There is no
way to provide adequate coverage of what has taken place. The e-mails
you have just read show yet another aspect of the problem. A reporter
obtains what seems to be an accurate statement from an individual who
should be aware of the details. There is no time to double-check. There
is likely no one available who wants to bother to correct errors with so
much critical activity taking place. Then we look like fools and still have
to take the time to accurately counter what has been stated.

Hurricane Katrina and similar disasters create additional concerns.
Say that a thousand people are dead and the number is too large to
comprehend. Show one body being removed while a loved one grieves at
the side of a rescue worker and it tears at your heart. News people want
to show the dead, whether it is a single image or the efforts to remove
large numbers of victims. The visual is almost as powerful as the classic
concept of putting a story of local violence at the top of the news hour,
what is derisively but accurately termed "If it bleeds, it leads."

We faced the concern of trying to respect the dead, respect those
who were grieving over an unexpected loss, keep the press away from
areas where rescue workers were trying to deal with both life and death,
and not seem as though we were orchestrating a cover-up. This situation became worse as the days passed and the media did what was their
right to do—brought a civil suit to be allowed to move about the Gulf
states unimpeded. If you followed the story of Katrina, you were probably aware of the media concerns. Appendix 1 takes you behind the
scenes and shows, through some e-mail exchanges, the reported stories,
the legal decision, and how we were responding to the suit at the same

time we were concerned with helping the survivors who had mostly been dispersed to other regions.

Under both the best and worst of circumstances, access by media professionals is critical for understanding one's neighborhood, city, state, nation, and the world. At the same time, there is a point when the media must realize that it is necessary to mentally take a step back and really look at the situation they are covering.

One of the most consistent criticisms I received toward the end of my tenure with the government was that I was too accessible. Why was I appearing on various news shows, giving interviews seemingly to anyone who asked, and meeting with the leaders of groups not necessarily influential in the city and with its recovery? This was in contrast to previous criticism that I was aloof and disrespectful toward the media by focusing on recovery and evacuation instead of talking with reporters.

Not that I was alone in all this. The reality of both Katrina and the other disasters I had covered in the previous few years was that everyone has a clearly defined interest and no one wants to be thwarted. I wanted New Orleans evacuated. I wanted to shake some sense into the heads of local and regional officials within Louisiana who delayed taking decisive action. I wanted to be left alone to do my job successfully by not veering from the methods of the past, even if there were new protocols among the agencies. The President wanted to enjoy his vacation while others took responsibility for an event coming slowly enough that he seemed able to pretend it wasn't going to be very serious.

* * *

There were other inappropriate events happening at the same time, though those of us in the field would not know about them until long after the fact. Perhaps the most interesting of the newly available stories was revealed by *GQ* magazine's Robert Draper, author of *Dead Certain: The Presidency of George W. Bush*. In an article in the June 2009 issue, he included this account:

> A final story of Rumsfeld's intransigence begins on Wednesday, August 31, 2005. Two days after Hurricane Katrina made landfall in New Orleans—and the same day that Bush viewed the damage on a flyover from his Crawford, Texas, retreat back to Washington—a White House advance team toured the devasta-

tion in an Air Force helicopter. Noticing that their chopper was outfitted with a search-and-rescue lift, one of the advance men said to the pilot, "We're not taking you away from grabbing people off of rooftops, are we?"

"No, sir," said the pilot. He explained that he was from Florida's Hurlburt Field Air Force base—roughly 200 miles from New Orleans—which contained an entire fleet of search-and-rescue helicopters. "I'm just here because you're here," the pilot added. "My whole unit's sitting back at Hurlburt, wondering why we're not being used."

The search-and-rescue helicopters were not being used because Donald Rumsfeld had not yet approved their deployment—even though, as Lieutenant General Russ Honoré, the cigar-chomping commander of Joint Task Force Katrina, would later tell me, "that Wednesday, we needed to evacuate people. The few helicopters we had in there were busy, and we were trying to deploy more."

And three years later, when I asked a top White House official how he would characterize Rumsfeld's assistance in the response to Hurricane Katrina, I found out why. "It was commonly known in the West Wing that there was a battle with Rumsfeld regarding this," said the official. "I can't imagine another defense secretary throwing up the kinds of obstacles he did." ("And He Shall Be Judged")

* * *

Many members of the media, both new reporters and those who were experienced, saw the potential for winning awards, winning raises, perhaps jumping from television reporter to television anchor, from blog commentator to magazine staffer. They wanted the visuals of the pain, suffering, and loss. They wanted the isolated stories of families in pain. They wanted to ride along on rescue boats. They wanted to show themselves as serious, reasoned, insightful—and having the story others could not get. The former meant they could be a hindrance to our efforts, working for the camera and not the best interests of the people in crisis. The latter meant they were desperate for exclusive interviews and could be vicious when they didn't receive them.

Unfortunately this often resulted in inaccurate accounts of the events and a lack of perception concerning the strengths and limitations of everyone involved.

AND THEN THERE WAS *TIME* . . .

My last media story is intensely personal, extremely upsetting to discuss even now, and makes no sense whatsoever. *Time* magazine's September 8 issue carried an article about me, challenging my credentials, my suitability for the work I was doing, and the integrity of the information available about me.

Perhaps I was the victim of the new demands of journalism on the men and women who cover the news. If you are constantly fighting to be first with the new, if you are trying to fill space in a magazine, space in the electronic version of the same publication, and space on an Internet site, there is little time for fact-checking.

Thirty years ago, when celebrities were fighting back against innuendo, misinformation, and outright lies in the popular press, *Time*'s fact-checkers were held to be the gold standard against which everyone else who cared measured themselves. This ranged from daily newspapers to such disparate publications as *Hustler* and the *National Enquirer*. [There was a period where, for reasons I never understood, *Hustler* combined serious journalism on important topics in the news. It is doubtful that anyone buying the magazine cared about such stories, but within the seemingly schizophrenic publishing company, the fact-checkers were highly skilled and discussed trying to be as good as or better than *Time* staff. The supermarket tabloid *National Enquirer* made certain its reporters tape recorded interviews and telephone calls, and then had fact-checkers follow up.]

In 2005, perhaps because of a change in standards, perhaps because of political pressure, perhaps because news was happening so fast that everyone wanted to be first more than anyone wanted to be accurate, something went horribly wrong and I was the victim. Instead of an attempt at objectivity, a determination to confirm all sides to a story and be certain they were presented, the "standard" for some in the media was outright bias.

The story *Time* did on me was not fact-checked nor did it make any corrections even though at least one of their sources, Claudia Deakins from Oklahoma, insisted that the reporter got the information wrong and demanded a correction. Instead, the reporter approached me while I was in the midst of the post-Katrina nightmare, sleeping little and disregarding everything except what needed to be done in the Gulf region. I was asked to provide my résumé for the story the magazine was writing.

My résumé?

You prepare a résumé when you're looking for a job. You don't send it out when you're in the middle of a natural disaster and responsible for coordinating an effective response. You don't carry one in your wallet or your car. You don't even think about it.

Time magazine wanted it, though. And they wanted it now. And I told them no. So they sulked and went home and showed me what they could do. They assassinated me in an article that was not immediate news; the article could have been delayed until either I could get them what they requested or they could do their own research.

"*Time* did four things," according to former U.S. Magistrate Judge Andy Lester, among other things a member of the 1980 Reagan transition team. "It claimed that Brown's position in Edmond, Oklahoma's city government was that of an intern, not someone with 'emergency management oversight'; that he hadn't been an adjunct professor; that he hadn't been a director of Oklahoma Christian Homes; and that his first boss after law school didn't think much of his legal abilities. To make the accusation fit, *Time* twisted Edmond city spokesperson Claudia Deakins's comments. Deakins has complained bitterly about *Time*'s inaccuracies; *Time* hasn't printed a retraction. Brown has documentary proof refuting all of *Time*'s charges, including affidavits, letters, even reviews he was given by the former boss *Time* quotes, who had called Brown 'an asset to the firm,' and described Brown's work as 'excellent,' 'first rate,' and 'outstanding.' But in the midst of America's worst natural disaster, *Time* gave Brown, who was still in Louisiana coordinating the response to Katrina, only 45 minutes to respond to its error-filled story. Within hours of its publication, media everywhere cited the *Time* piece as gospel and Brown was sent back to Washington. He resigned on Monday."

I was actually ready to quit without the hassle. I had been warned that I was going to be made the scapegoat for all failures. In fact, I was told that during a cabinet meeting someone, allegedly Donald Rumsfeld, the secretary of defense, had noticed that the press was beating up on me. He reportedly said they should do something to help me since they were all fully aware of my accomplishments and willingness to take responsibility where mistakes were made. However, the President shot down that idea. He felt it was better that the media beat me up than attack him.

There were other indicators of what was happening, of course, including specially assigned, highly skilled public relations personnel being loaned to me and then withdrawn when it seemed they might be effective. It was a little like working successfully in an office for years, then one day arriving and finding your nameplate on the door is misspelled. The next day your file cabinet is missing, the files stacked on the desk. The day after, the desk is missing. The day after that . . . You get the idea. Eventually you are in an empty room where no one can find you, no one consults you, and the only person you see in the hallway who is walking in your direction is carrying severance papers.

It was time for me to go.

CHAPTER 12

YOU LIVE *WHERE?*

HAMBURGERS DON'T KILL PEOPLE, HOT DOGS DO

THE STORY came across my desk at the radio station where I have a news/talk show. A woman who had suffered the horrendous loss of a child was on a crusade to save the lives of children throughout the United States.

It was every parent's nightmare. Her child had put a seemingly harmless substance into his mouth, apparently while no one else was in the room, only to discover that deadly objects can come in attractive packages sold in neighborhood supermarkets. Before anyone could reach him, the child had died from eating a seemingly innocuous hot dog. Instead of taking small bites, he had put it in his mouth at such an angle that it lodged in his throat, choking and suffocating him. The grieving mother's crusade, one mentioned in newspapers and radio and television news shows around the country, was to demand that the government order a change in the design of the hot dog. The traditional sausage shape, as she now saw it, was a potential killer.

No, I am not making this up. I am also not telling you this as a joke. I have children, and when they were small, I shared every parent's fears. Will a game of chase in the front yard result in one of my kids running into the street just as a car drives down the block? Will my neighbor backing out of the driveway see my child riding her bicycle on the sidewalk? Is the car driving slowly down the street being driven by an ultra-safety-conscious fellow parent or by someone who wishes to harm my children?

Some parental fears are valid, of course. Some seem extreme until we read about some other parent experiencing the unspeakable. The fact that the incident might have happened in Connecticut while my family was living in Colorado, that it made the news because it was unusual, does not matter. We fear random violence simply because it is random; my wife and I could be reading about a stranger's child, but a stranger and his wife could be reading about ours—unlikely, but still possible.

Like every other parent, I did what I felt was necessary to protect my children on their way from being toddlers to establishing their own adult lives. I insisted that they wear helmets when riding a bicycle. I stressed that they should never ride in the street. I talked about watching out for cars since the driver might be distracted. I talked about "stranger danger" and saying no to drugs. I probably sounded like the messages being taught on a *Barney & Friends* video, especially when I gave the same warnings to my teenagers.

The truth is that concern for those we love is a part of being able to love. We are driven to protect just as we are driven to nurture. And for the most part we are successful. Most of our children grow into adulthood. They survive illness, accidents, violence in the streets, drunk drivers, experimentation with alcohol, and all the other things we warned them about. And the majority of those children who achieve adult independence will outlive us, a cycle of life we consider normal.

Death is also normal, though it is often considered indelicate to mention this fact. I don't mean death from old age or death from a traffic accident. I don't mean death in wartime or in the midst of a disaster. Such deaths are a reality, of course, but children also die. Babies can be stillborn. Toddlers can have fatal heart conditions, leukemia, or any number of other health crises for which we have no cure. They can have juvenile onset diabetes. Or undetected food allergies, medication allergies, and slowly developing genetic problems. The list goes on and on, and while some things are within our control, others are not, especially the totally unexpected.

That is why children even die eating a hot dog.

I will admit that I find the crusade to change hot dogs both under-standable and outrageous. The mother has supporters and she certainly is getting attention from the media. But hot dogs? There are millions, perhaps billions of hot dogs and sausages eaten every year. They are chewed. They are swallowed. And the diners, regardless of their ages, go on about their lives without another thought. Yet to the mother whose toddler died, the hot dog is a deadly weapon—lethal matter disguised as food. She is probably certain not only that some other child will die if she doesn't bring attention to the issue, but also that the only way she can give meaning to her child's brief life is by alerting the public to the danger.

And now, if you will forgive me for sounding callous or diminishing the mother's pain, I have one simple question. So what?

You may think that I am going to go off on a tirade about the fear of hot dogs. You may think that I am going to make jokes about the incident. Neither is true. I mention the hot dog because it presents a clear understanding of how humans can feel overwhelmed by life's risks. So much happens in life that is out of our control that we often obsess over the relatively meaningless if we think we can control it.

We become fixated on a minor incident that is scary, but an aberration, and ignore the meaningful concerns that are beyond our ability to control. Or we become overwhelmed in the face of a crisis and play the blame game. Finally, we start crusades, so that "no one else ever experiences what I did."

THE BLAME GAME

I worked in a Republican administration. I am writing this book during a Democratic administration. This means that Republicans temporarily on the outside are writing the self-serving and revisionist stories of what took place while they were in power just as, during the previous administration, the Democrats did the same. It is only natural and serves the public in several different ways.

First, it is very likely that while events are taking place, events we now consider history, all the facts are not available. Perhaps the people involved are too close to events unraveling on their watch to look beyond their immediate concerns. Perhaps the event is being handled on multiple fronts and it is necessary to step back to fully comprehend it.

WHAT IS RISK?

We face two types of risk each day. There is the risk we anticipate and the risk we ignore. Usually the deadlier of the two is the risk we ignore. That is the risk I refer to when I speak of deadly indifference.

If you have small children, the two types of risk are evident in how we plan our living arrangements. We look at our home from the vantage point of a curious child with no understanding of which objects can hurt and which are harmless. Knives and other dangerous objects in our kitchen are put high in cupboards or locked in drawers. We install smoke detectors and plan for how we will safely evacuate our home in the event of a fire. We don't let the children play without an adult or responsible sitter watching them. These are risks we anticipate, sharing our concerns with other parents as we discuss "childproofing" our homes.

Other risks make us so uncomfortable that we ignore them. We teach our children about "stranger danger," yet the majority of child molestations occur within families by people children know and trust.

Law enforcement statistics show that people who want to teach, nurture, and protect children are drawn to the same professions as those who want to molest them. The best and the worst among us are teachers and pastors, Scout leaders and coaches, police officers and firefighters, men and women, straight and gay. They all hold positions that make us feel we should instinctively trust them. Parents all share discomfort over the possibility that there is a deviant "good guide" in the lives of our children and our families, so we do not look for that exception. We are indifferent to the risk until an incident occurs, and even then we tend to see it as an exception.

We may say that we are different, that we don't take unnecessary risks. I, personally, would never want to live in that section of New Orleans where I witnessed the rising water, the fires, and the other horrors that could have been avoided by living on higher ground. At the same time, I live in an area of Colorado that experiences periodic wildfires, some so severe that law enforcement officers go door to door to tell us to evacuate. I keep travel kits ready that contain various items I will need to get through several days' evacuation—clothing, food for our animals, medications, and the like. I brag about how quickly my wife and I can grab our bags, place the dogs in the cars, and drive away from the fire danger. To my way of thinking, we are prepared for the unexpected. To those who choose to live elsewhere, we are indifferent to the seriousness of the risks. All of us choose indifference at one time or another, and I am not all that different from the people of the Gulf region who live too close to areas that are prone to natural disasters.

* * *

A few years ago British emergency management and homeland security officials approached me to undertake a mission during which I would discuss disaster education with several top officials in the United Kingdom. They had watched tsunami devastation, flooding from hurricanes, and other natural disasters create increasing havoc in nations throughout the world, yet the British leadership had a tradition of never educating the public about natural disasters. They had strong programs to prevent and combat terrorism, whether from political or religious extremist organizations. But Britain, an island country, was admitting for the first time that not only were there areas vulnerable to devastation from flooding, they had never tried to educate the public about the risks and any possible preventive measures. They contacted me after seeing that in the United States we did make some effort to alert the public and wondered what they could do.

I flew to London, had the conference, and outlined what should have been countrywide concerns. The problem was that there were no floods at the time, and a lack of recent crises lowers the priority of any government or public action. So when flooding did occur a few years later in the areas we had discussed, electric power plants stopped functioning. The fire brigades had no coordinated plan in place to utilize critical professionals and moved them among one another's jurisdictions as needed; so much needless damage occurred that the Home Office finally faced the crisis we had earlier discussed. The result was the Pitt report and the first hesitant steps to educate the British public about the periodic natural disasters the island nation had been vulnerable to for centuries. While I won't quote it here, to understand Britain's indifference, you only need to see the titles of the 505-page report on massive floods in 2007, floods for which the island country was not prepared. Among the areas covered were

Knowing when and where it will flood

Improved planning and reducing the risk of flooding and its impact

Being rescued and cared for in an emergency

Maintaining power and water supplies and protecting essential services

Protecting families and homes

Recovery

There was more, eight sections in all, but what is amazing are two realities. England went through hell during the early days of World War II when the Germans were bombing London nightly. The young men and women who had survived in the shelters and often signed up with the army moved into positions of power and authority, yet flooding, a greater and more frequent risk than wartime, was never addressed.

The second reality is that England has always been an island nation. It didn't magically separate from mainland Europe. Generations were born, grew old, and died on the island. Yet the Pitt report, released less than three years ago as I write this, was the first serious effort to address the risk of flooding that I am aware of. Again, familiarity breeds indifference, and indifference can turn deadly.

* * *

I was involved with FEMA's response to the terrorist attacks on 9/11 at the Pentagon and New York City's World Trade Center Towers. More than three thousand people died in what was then the worst attack against Americans in our country.

This was not the first time airplanes were used as missiles to destroy lives and property. Joseph Kennedy Jr., the brother of Jack, Bobby, and Teddy, was killed during World War II in an accident related to just such aircraft use.

Guided missiles were under development but the Allied forces needed an immediate way to better attack enemy targets. The answer for the Army Air Corps was to load an airplane with explosives with a trigger that had to be rigged at the last minute. A volunteer pilot would fly toward the target, perhaps a factory, military installation, railroad yard, or other location critical for the enemy. A chase plane would follow, equipped with radio controls to take over the flight of the front plane. Then the first pilot would set the electronics needed for the plane to smash into its target (or as close as it could get since the technology was crude), leap from the aircraft and parachute to safety. The chase plane would use the remote to send the front plane to its target and then stay to rescue the downed pilot.

The mission was always a volunteer one because everything about the airplane-as-missile was crude and carried with it the chance for a deadly accident. That was the circumstance with Joe Kennedy Jr., who was killed when the plane exploded before he could jump from the aircraft.

More than five decades later there were many in government, especially within the state of New York, who were more concerned about another airplane-as-missile assault than they were guided missile assaults. A guided missile was a weapon related to a country going to war. Our military and intelligence services could likely anticipate such a crisis and head it off in some way. But hijackers going through routine airport security and willing to ride the plane to their deaths in addition to the deaths of countless others were a concern the officials wanted to address.

The problem was not the idea that there could be an attack on other tall buildings in Manhattan. Instead, the concern was with the Indian Point atomic power plant in Buchanan, New York. The plant was close enough to Manhattan Island that if it somehow exploded, radiation from the blast would contaminate all of New York City, killing millions and leaving it uninhabitable for centuries to come. Then, depending upon the wind currents, other states and parts of Canada might be affected by levels of radiation high enough to shorten lives or cause certain types of cancer. Would I quietly and without alerting the public learn if Indian Point was vulnerable to a plane smashing into the top of the reactor?

I had engineers, atomic scientists, meteorologists, and others explore what could happen at Indian Point. When all the tests and analyses were completed, the answer was a relief to those requesting the study. A direct hit into the reactor would not create a problem.

And with that information I was told, in effect, thank you very much. We don't need anything further.

But . . . I said.

Thank you. Now go do something else, they responded.

But . . .

There would be nothing more, however. I did what was asked. The results pleased them. So what was the problem? The tests also showed that a handful of men or women could *walk* into or infiltrate the plant, bypassing security, and take control of Indian Point or set explosives on the ground that would create havoc, potentially causing a radiation leak, and perhaps rendering parts of New York City a dead zone.

* * *

From my journal July 18, 2003:

Before I left Washington today I had a meeting with Hillary Clinton. A couple of weeks ago FEMA/DHS made the decision that the evacuation and emergency plans at the Indian Point nuclear power plant in Westchester County, New York, were adequate and that we had "reasonable assurance" that the plans would work. It was a very controversial decision as many fringe environmental groups, and some reasonable groups, I suppose, had decided this was their target and if attacked will cause a catastrophic event. The Nuclear Regulatory Commission doesn't believe that, and they're the experts. I don't believe that, and endorsed the staff decision to determine the plans adequate. This was done only after a review of the plans and an ongoing exercise of the plans.

Anyway, the senator and I met today in private. We each had a staff person present, and for the first time, she really opened up, both personally and about her views on the plant.

Publicly she has stated that our decision was flawed, our process corrupt, and that she had grave concerns about our decision. In private, she almost apologetically provided a letter to me outlining information she wanted, a request for congressional hearing support, etc. But privately, she made it clear and unequivocal she understood the plant probably shouldn't be closed, that if it were power rates would skyrocket. She also acknowledged that some of the groups opposing the decision were simply trying to shut the plant down, regardless of the merits of the evacuation/emergency plans. She was surprisingly candid with me.

As the discussion became more about "how are you doing" kind of stuff, she laughed about the "Washington timeline" and how long it takes to get things done. She talked about the rumors and stories about her, and proceeded to show me the front page of a tabloid newspaper that claimed in bold headlines, "Hillary Has Child by Alien" or something like that. We laughed about it and I told her I'd like a copy of the newspaper article signed by her. She thought that would be hilarious.

Security concerns could be addressed. Changes could be instigated. The public could be protected. All the government had to do was acknowledge the problem. This was one they felt they had no control over and so didn't want to think about it. They became indifferent because this was the risk that seemed too great to tackle.

These comments are not meant to attack politicians. When some people feel overwhelmed, they often become indifferent to danger. With others, there is another factor. They look at what has *not* happened and dismiss the likelihood that something terrible will happen in their lifetime, even in an area where danger may be indicated. And then there are those who overreact.

I still remember what happened on December 3, 2001, when I attended the Western Governors' Association meeting in El Paso, Texas, when Gary Johnson, governor of New Mexico, spoke about his experience.

* * *

Journal entry, December 4, 2001:

He [Governor Johnson] *talked about his experience being in the Atlanta airport when someone "breached" security by running down an up-escalator as he sought to retrieve his camera and get back to his waiting son. Gary spoke about the need to weigh risk and the degree of risk we're willing to accept. He described how, after the breach occurred, rumors flew through the evacuated passengers, claiming someone had a gun, that someone had a machine gun and had gunned down security people. He laughed about how flights that had taxied to the runway and were ready to take off were halted. Over 27,000 people were evacuated from an airport for this one incident. He questions whether we're willing to make those kinds of sacrifices for security.*

But the greater point he made was the message we were sending to potential terrorists. Namely, they can shut down our transportation system without really doing much. Create a chaotic situation, brandish a gun, make a threat, jump a turnstile, and you can shut down an entire international airport for hours, disrupt travel across the country, and not really expend any capital or resources doing so. Eventually people will become so frustrated that they will stop flying.

Later I talked about my own experience. I had traveled to El Paso from Washington, but because of my government position I had to make stops along the way—Chicago, Denver, and Albuquerque, a circuitous route to the border town I was about to leave. My unusual route was a valid reason for concern at the check-in counter; however, I thought all would be resolved when I pulled out my national security credentials with photo identification, badge, and other proof of my authority. But as I noted:

My checked bag was hand searched anyway. What did they do? They dug through and removed almost all of my clothes and files, and did things like squeeze my toothpaste. They looked at my razor. They thumbed through my files.

The men who handled the search were nice to me and thought that I should not have been stopped given my provable position with the government. They thanked me personally and for FEMA because they felt we were doing a good job, even if there was the occasional silliness of a search. What none of us could imagine was what happened when I reached the gate in the boarding area and the questions it raised about real airport security:

Going through the magnetometer in El Paso, my briefcase caught the eye of the screener (which it never has before, and I'm carrying the same things I always carry). They first checked the bag for explosives by running the test that checks for residue (I don't know the name of the device or test, but they swab the handle or inside with a cloth which is then run through a spectrograph). After that was negative, they then decide to do a hand check of the bag's contents. What does that entail? It means they took my Mont Blanc ink pens and checked to see they had ink in them. They looked through the biography of Theodore Roosevelt, they rifled through the pocket with my handy-wipes and aspirin. They looked at my keys. They did not open or check my cell phone to see if it worked. They did not open the box of Altoids to see if I had something in there. They did not pull out the cables I use to connect my cell phone to my computer. They did, however, stick their hand down in my change pocket.

All of which caused me to wonder. Why are keys allowed on airplanes, but only plastic knives allowed with meals? Why are metal forks allowed but metal boxes not opened? Why are National Guard troops stationed at screening stations when none of the terrorists on September 11th carried a firearm? What balance have we achieved in our security checkpoints that has resulted in incremental increase in airline security? None, in my opinion. . . . It just seems to me that we're wasting resources, not improving security, and creating both a false sense of security while not really doing anything to stop a terrorist or, for that matter, just a nut who wants to hijack an airplane with his sharp keys or dinner fork.

* * *

New Orleans is a city mostly below sea level. That was true before Hurricane Katrina. That is true today, several years after the storm. If you live in New Orleans, you either rent or buy on the highest ground, or you might die.

There, I said it. Live in the wrong section of New Orleans and you might die. Rebuild the city to its grandeur pre-Katrina, and guess what?

You might die. Humans do not control hurricanes and I, personally, do not believe these are divine storms that the holy and sanctified can experience without risk.

Worse in the case of New Orleans was what was revealed in the September 1, 2005, issue of the *New York Times* in which writers Andrew C. Revkin and Christopher Drew reported: "The 17th Street levee that gave way and led to the flooding of New Orleans was part of an intricate, aging system of barriers and pumps that was so chronically underfinanced that senior regional officials of the Army Corps of Engineers complained about it publicly for years." Most New Orleans residents knew of the problem. It hadn't failed them yet, though, so rather than being proactive, they were mostly indifferent.

The same is true of those regions of the United States where there are earthquake faults. Residents of Los Angeles joke about "the big one," referring to an earthquake of such magnitude that it will topple buildings and elevated highways. For years experts in the field have explained that it is only a matter of time before a quake such as the one that hit Chile in 2010 strikes the even more populated California city. But still people move to the region, stay in the region, and continue to overlook the inevitable.

Why do they act so foolishly? Why do any of us act so foolishly? Why are we indifferent to the risks of where we choose to live and what we choose to do? Because a problem hasn't happened yet, either in our lifetime or since we considered where and how we wish to live. Somehow we believe that if we have not had a particular experience, the chances of it happening in the immediate future are lessened.

Some cities sit on what are known as hundred-year floodplains. Supposedly this is an area where once every hundred years heavy rains and the angle of natural drainage combine to create a flood that will destroy everything in its path.

Just the term "hundred-year floodplain" sounds remarkably scientific. "Obviously" records have been kept year after year, decade after decade, and century after century. "Obviously" the developers have used these records when planning where to place buildings. "Obviously" such ideas are nonsense. Rarely do records go back more than one hundred years. In addition, just the statement "about once in a hundred years" is meaningless. No one knows when such floods will occur, only that they have occurred and will again. We do far better in recognizing hurricane and tornado seasons, yet even they are not predictable as to dates or intensity. However, we tell ourselves that the hundred-year floodplain is real because it is an area where we want to live or work.

You buy a new car and find a maintenance schedule in the handbook that comes with it. The time for getting an oil change approaches but you are busy. You decide to put it off because the car's been running well and you see no reason for worry. There is a question about the brakes because each time you apply them quickly, the car seems to pull ever so slightly to the right. Maybe there's something wrong with the steering mechanism. More likely the problem is with an underinflated tire. It can wait.

But finally there are some problems. You hear a high-pitched whine that a friend says might be the fan belt, whatever that is. The "check engine" light comes on. And then the car stops working. You have the car towed to a repair shop where the cost of your delayed maintenance is far more than you anticipated. And when the mechanic asks if you noticed that something was wrong with the car, you say that it had been working just fine, that nothing seemed amiss. We ignore regular maintenance because we haven't had any problems. We are indifferent to the familiar.

* * *

Journal entry:

> *What is the actual danger of terrorism? How many people are killed in car accidents today? How many people will be murdered today by someone they know? How many people will die of AIDS, lung cancer, drug overdoses, or other self-inflicted diseases from their lifestyle? I need to find those numbers, because I venture to say that almost every one of them might be more than were killed by terrorism.*
>
> *Are we playing into the hands of the terrorists by our threat announcements, by the presence of the National Guard troops at airports, by the absolute war-zone-like enhancements we've placed around government buildings? Again, what is the proper balance between security and risk?*

The most serious example of deadly indifference in our daily lives is when we choose to invest our fears in areas that frighten us yet seem within our ability to control. What is the chance that an enemy nation or a terrorist will detonate a bomb that leaves a million people homeless? What is the chance that the bomb will destroy thousands of acres of wilderness land? What is the chance that thousands of people will die with no way to either escape their fate or fight back?

I don't have the answer. You don't have the answer. All we can do is rely on intelligence gathering on a local, regional, national, and international scale. And we can buy weapons; then master their use and make certain that everyone who lives with us has the same mastery, not to mention their own handguns for when they leave the house.

We know that there can be danger on aircraft and that we cannot bring a weapon on board. Perhaps we can learn unarmed self-defense in case of a hijacking or terrorist. Certainly we can constantly watch our fellow passengers, being ever ready to alert the flight attendants as we heroically attack the bad guys. Probably we should simply skip flying and take a train or a bus. We could also drive because the car can probably handle the trip before we have to have a tune-up. There is a good chance that we can carry a weapon on other forms of transportation, even if we have to keep it in our luggage.

We become hypervigilant. Is someone following us? Is someone taking pictures with a cell phone camera in an area that seems appropriate for a terrorist attack? Is someone who looks as though he's from the Middle East wearing a beard? We heard that when a man decides to become a terrorist, he grows a beard. Or is it that he grows a beard, and when he decides to become a terrorist he shaves it off, so we have to look for clean-shaven Middle Easterners?

Then we add the necessary accessories—a GPS navigational system we can use to find our way and to ensure that we can be found in a crisis. We carry a cell phone unless we're in wilderness areas where we also carry a high-powered citizens band radio to keep us connected with truckers, state highway patrol officers, and county sheriffs. We have the hand-crank emergency radio. We have tactical flashlights that are weatherproof, can take physical abuse, and have a beam that can be seen a mile or more away. We have . . . You get the idea.

Control. These are all items and precautions that help us stay in control. Terrorists killed more than three thousand people at the World Trade Towers in New York City, but some people won't live in New York City, or visit there if they can avoid it. We know where to live, how to live, and are prepared for danger we can control by our actions.

But what about life's other realities? What about forest fires that occur both naturally and accidentally? What about influenza, which comes in a variety of unpredictable and mutating strains? For that matter, what about the next Hurricane Katrina, wherever it may land?

We have no real control over such matters. We can plan long and hard. We can answer the difficult questions about what we need to do to protect the residents most likely to be impacted by earthquakes, floods, hurricanes, and volcanoes.

SO WHAT IS THE ANSWER?

There is no single answer to the problem of deadly indifference and how it narrows our thinking about an impending natural disaster such as Hurricane Katrina. The nature of humanity is such that we seem to emotionally survive by compartmentalizing danger. We exercise control where we think we can influence the outcome of an encounter with the unexpected—a skyjacking, terrorists sneaking across our borders, access to the secrets of the atomic bomb, and so on. And we become indifferent to events we have no control over even though advanced planning could save lives.

Cities can't stop infrastructure failures, storms, and conflagrations. But cities, and the people who live there, can plan for the unavoidable uncontrollable realities of life. They cannot have evacuation plans only for the core city, much in the manner that cities with large, popular college and professional sports teams plan the best and fastest ways to move people from the stadium to their homes after a well-attended game; they must also think beyond the suburbs. They can look to see where an entire city could be evacuated and how the sudden, overwhelming numbers of evacuees can be housed and fed where they have traveled. Plans can be made for regional stockpiling in the manner of

FEMA. Thought should be given to how several hundred thousand people will function in a location miles from their homes.

First responders and the public in general can be educated about the beliefs of people from various cultures living in the United States. Currently we rely on old movies, horror and crime novels, teachers with only slightly more knowledge than their students, and the like to learn not only about the different forms of Islam, for example, but also about Judaism and Christianity. All religious groups have rites and rituals no one has reason to fear. Likewise, all religious groups have a small number of violent extremists who will harm others in the name of God as they interpret God through a twisted theology.

Deadly indifference is a human trait, not just one that relates to this country or one political party. It is a way to feel safe, secure, as though the uncontrollable aspects of life don't need to be considered. But we must never forget that such thinking is both normal and an ever present danger to our safety if we ignore its reality. The lessons of Hurricane Katrina and the numerous other disasters that occur in some part of the world every day should be ones we accept as reflecting the human condition, even as we seek ways to better prepare for the unwanted and unexpected.

AFTERWORD

THROUGHOUT *Deadly Indifference* you have read excerpts from a journal I maintained during the time I was working for President George W. Bush. I never expected that I would need to use the entries to verify my experiences. I maintained it for two reasons. The first was that working for the White House is one of the loneliest jobs a family-oriented man or woman can have. The President essentially lives in his office building; the White House has areas where the President works and areas that are private, reserved solely for family and anyone they choose to entertain. Some trips the President must handle alone, but these are relatively few and for a short duration. My job took me throughout the world, always apart from my wife and children, always in the midst of some of the greatest crises to impact our nation and the world. The work was exciting, demanding, and made meaningful communication with my family almost impossible for days or weeks at a time.

Each day that I traveled, with the exception of those days when the intensity of the work overwhelmed me, such as the immediate aftermath of the 9/11 attacks, I wrote about what was happening, the details of meetings, and even my decision process at the time. Sometimes I was successful and it was with pride that I noted what had happened. Sometimes I failed, either because I made mistakes or because the best judgment call at the time was not good enough. I always noted the details. I am only human, and if anyone knows how human we are, it is those people closest to us. To exaggerate would have defeated my effort to share my life with those who matter most.

The second reason I maintained the journal was that writing is my way of thinking. Putting down not only my thoughts but the details of what is taking place day to day helps me understand what I need to be doing now and in the future relative to the current situation.

Eventually my journal reached several hundred pages and included copies of some e-mails, articles in major publications showing an outsider's view of what was happening, and myriad other details. I suppose I thought that one day my wife would read this and understand why I had agreed to take a job that would cause so much emotional turmoil when we were separated. I thought that my children might be interested, and if not my children, their spouses or my grandchildren. Whatever the case, the entries were thorough and I expected to keep them private.

Then, four years after I left the Bush White House, I started writing this book. Around the same time there were high government officials, especially advisers to the president, who began writing about their time in office. However, what became obvious was that the information was often in conflict.

Hurricane Katrina was a disaster on many levels. Every participant has his or her own version of the almost heroic personal actions taken in a desperate race to beat the storm, protect the people, and blame FEMA. One person talks of demanding supplies critical for the people who had evacuated to the Superdome, for example. However, that person never mentioned that the Superdome—twelve feet below water level and protected only when the levees are maintained—was never part of the initial planning. A mandatory evacuation of New Orleans should have been ordered earlier based on the information available to all officials weeks and more ahead of the storm's landfall.

There were other mistakes, but ultimately it has been easiest to attack a handful of us who were in the trenches at the time. Our critics, often powerful men who helped guide the President despite having been only minimally a part of the planning or the aftermath, try to take full responsibility for all that worked and attack others for what did not.

Two things have enabled these officials turned self-serving autobiographers to spin the details of the past. The first is the simple fact that most people do not know what should have happened. They do not know the planning that was involved. They do not know the options available and rejected by high officials whose frequent indecision and occasional bad choices changed a serious situation into a needlessly deadly one. And they do not know the bias against those on the lowest level of socioeconomic existence.

The second thing has been the lack of available documentation, either because the self-serving wanted facts that contradicted their statements to be hidden or because, by the time records were made public, months had passed. Interest in a disaster diminishes dramatically in the days that follow the time of greatest impact. The discovery of videotape of White House conferences, reports issued as a result of congressional investigations, and other data that show the accuracy of what is written in this book were underreported. Fortunately, they are readily available, have not been classified, and can be found with a little searching on the Internet.

The problem is that the average person is not going to search the Internet looking for either objective reporting or indisputable facts in order to draw his or her own conclusions. Such effort is time-consuming and requires careful analysis of the sources for the material, not just the material itself (e.g., Wikipedia entries are not valid historical documents. Neither are websites and blogs meant solely to propagate one idea or another).

In the end we are left with a "he said/she said/he said/she said" approach to what happened during Hurricane Katrina. Some of the statements are true. Some are false. And some of the statements are self-serving creations. Counter them and you appear to be trying to save face after a failure. Don't counter them and "obviously" your accuser is accurate.

As I write this, Karl Rove, perhaps President Bush's most important adviser, is using his book and media appearances to, among other things, show my failings during Katrina. Other public officials are discussed, too, but only they can speak for what they did or did not do. In addition, other books are being written that may have sections like Rove's in which facts are presented but with whatever spin is in the best interest of the author.

President Bush, in his book, writes that Michael Chertoff, Secretary of Homeland Security, told the President he had lost confidence in me and that I had become "insubordinate." Yes, I had. Michael Chertoff simply did not know how to respond to a disaster and was trying to micromanage our response to Hurricane Katrina from Washington, D.C. Chertoff would countermand decisions or orders I had given on the ground based on the information we had on-the-scene, which further exasperated federal, state, and local responders. His actions certainly heightened the importance of the question, who's in charge?

I chuckled to myself when I read that Chertoff told President Bush that he felt I had "frozen" under the pressure of the disaster. When a commander orders his troop leaders to stay in their bunkers, as Chertoff had done by ordering me to stay in my office in Baton Rouge, you no longer are capable of responding quickly and effectively. Chertoff had effectively frozen me in an office, cutting me off from those who most needed leadership and direction.

I tried to think how I could handle the problem. I have the various reports made by different investigative groups that support what I have written in this book. I was thinking of adding another appendix and including copies of these reports, which would have added another hundred or so pages to this book, bored you with their dryness, and incurred the wrath of my publisher for wasting paper.

Then I thought of my journal. This lengthy document, made as events were unfolding, tells the details, my thoughts, my successes, and my failures. It could have been written only in the midst of the events and it puts a very different lens to what is being said by those who would rather attack than admit they were human, too.

Throughout this book my journal entries provide a fly-on-the-wall view of critical planning sessions. It also shows my thinking as I had to deal with others, some hostile, some unprepared, and some supportive because they came to the same conclusions I did. Whatever the case, the journal is my way to counter misinformation with facts.

The journal is a contemporary narrative of my work and life experiences that I started in 1994. Only a very small portion of that journal is used in this book. Perhaps later, the stories it contains about the events of 9/11, the internal deliberations in the White House, and the eventual creation of that monstrosity, the Department of Homeland Security, will be edited and included in another book about events prior to Hurricane Katrina.

APPENDIX 1

BEHIND THE SCENES
What You Didn't Read, See, or Hear

AS I'VE TRIED to describe, Hurricane Katrina was a disaster on many levels, but what people found most difficult to understand was the dance between those of us assigned to save as many lives as possible and the media reporting possibly the biggest story of their careers. I covered some of the issues earlier; however, to truly understand agency thinking versus reporter desires, you'll need a glimpse behind the scenes:

From: Rule, Natalie
Sent: Wednesday, September 07, 2005 156 PM
To: hJ
Cc: Wing, Deborah; Kinerney, Eugene
Subject: RE: FEMA No Photos
Importance: High

This sound fine for follow up stories?

For rescue and recovery efforts, we cannot have them taking up needed space in vehicles and boats. From the standpoint of our mortuary operations, we will not assist media in viewing our operations out of respect for those who have perished in this storm and respect for their families.

Decisions about running footage or photos of what the media has filmed is up to them, but FEMA is being respectful of those who have lost their lives and of their families and will not allow filming of FEMA operations and certainly will not assist media in covering these operations.

* * *

Katrina's Aftermath
FEMA Wants No Photos of Dead

NEW ORLEANS, Sept 7, 2005 (Reuters)—The U.S. agency leading Hurricane Katrina rescue efforts said Tuesday that it does not want the news media to photograph the dead as they are recovered.

The Federal Emergency Management Agency, heavily criticized for its slow response to the devastation caused by the hurricane, rejected journalists' requests to accompany rescue boats searching for storm victims.

An agency spokeswoman said space was needed on the rescue boats.

"We have requested that no photographs of the deceased be made by the media," the spokeswoman said in an e-mail.

* * *

From: Baker, Jean
To: Taylor, Cindy; Ellis, Barbara J
Sent: Thu Sep 08 17:06:16 2005
Subject: Public Inquiry: Press Censorship

Cindy—this afternoon R6 got a call from a private citizen who wanted to register her concern about FEMA censoring the press by not allowing media to cover the recovery of the dead in LA and other affected areas. She specifically cited an article in today's *Washington Post* and a blog posting by NBC's Brian Williams; both say that FEMA and other authorities in New Orleans are preventing media from entering areas that were previously open to media, presumably to prevent coverage of recovery of bodies as the flood waters recede.

It would be helpful to know if FEMA has issued any guidance to reporters on their ability to cover this aspect of the recovery. The caller was told that FEMA Region VI is responding to a variety of media requests related to Katrina recovery and we hadn't heard of an all-out ban on any aspect of coverage.

* * *

From: Andrews, Nicol D–Public Affairs
Sent: Thursday, September 08, 2005 6.1 3 PM
To: Besanceney, Brian; Bergman, Cynthia; Rule, Natalie; Knocke, William R; Montgomery, Kathleen; Agen, Jarrod; Karonis, Jeff; Bahamonde, Marty; Taylor, Cindy
Subject: issues on the radar

There are several things that need to be on every one's radar–some are being addressed, others are still so fluid that we will want to stay on top of them operationally so we know when resolution is reached. Just wanted to make sure everyone was aware and what (as far as I know) is being done. Please add to and/or correct anything you know to be different than what is listed below:

1. Photos/film of deceased; we will not assist media in filming nor invite them to join DMORT operations out of respect for the deceased and their families.

2. DMORT operation; federal, state and local officials are working with Kenyon International to collect and process the bodies of victims throughout the hardest hit areas of Louisiana. Bodies are being treated with dignity and respect–once they are identified and processed, they are turned over to the state for notification of the next of kin. Right now, teams are gathering bodies that are in the open and will begin a more methodical grid driven search led by members of the 82nd Airborne in the next couple of days. No estimate yet as to how long this process will take.

3. Ongoing evacuation; Operations reports that rescue teams are still evacuating approximately 1,000 people per day from New Orleans and outlying parishes.

4. FEMA 'drivers' arrested; the Plaquemines Parish sheriff's office is claiming the arrest of two FEMA 'drivers' for looting. Logistics is working to confirm this report, assuming reference to contract personnel hired to transport commodities and supplies, not technically FEMA employees.

5. FEMA officials commandeering private property; several reports of various 'FEMA officials' commandeering private property for use in the response operation. FEMA does not have the legal authority to do this and suspicious activity should be reported immediately to the DHS IG fraud hotline. (It is worth noting that these kinds of reports are not uncommon following a disaster—people misrepresent themselves as FEMA for personal gain.) Several reports need to be knocked down as soon as possible with strong language that anyone misrepresenting themselves will be caught and prosecuted. Thought from front office here is a PSA campaign—know Marty was working on that.

6. Cruise ships; Ships in Texas are in the process of being moved to dock in Mississippi and Louisiana to house disaster relief workers in addition to land or rather than hurricane survivors. There are several updates to the housing situation that will likely be resolved later today. Stay tuned.

7. Debit cards expedited assistance; A great deal of confusion still exists regarding debit cards. These are a single tool for expedited assistance for those who do not have access to a bank account. Cards and PINS are issued simultaneously and the $2000 is immediately available upon receipt. Cindy has recommended a plan to address this issue nationally in addition to field press briefing this afternoon.

8. Lockdown at the Astrodome; Confusion and excitement about the announcement of expedited assistance created a security situation at the Astrodome where guards had to lock down the facility and secure the gates. For obvious reasons, state and local officials are concerned with how this program will proceed. FEMA is working with them currently to resolve.

9. Shelter Plan; expect a solid draft of the plan by today.

10. Pets; PETA has waged a campaign to include pets in the rescue operations. That organization is being tapped to help organize a mission to rescue pets alongside other ongoing operations. More on this tomorrow.

11. USS Comfort; If the ship can make it through the Pascagoula channel, the Comfort will dock in New Orleans with its full complement of medical providers to serve as a hospital. The ship has 250 hospital beds and 750 additional beds—most of the additional beds are used by support staff.

12. Positioning of travel trailers; the state of Louisiana is still in deliberations on a site or series of sites (like we did in Florida) to place somewhere

in the neighborhood of 10,000 travel trailers that will be made available for temporary housing.

13. Deployment of FEMA personnel; AP reported incorrectly that Brown waited until 911 to deploy 1,000 personnel. Story was driven by a single memo obtained by the AP that referred to our CR cadre. Issue addressed, but please be aware in case you see it running elsewhere.

14. Timeline; DHS is finalizing an official reconstruction of events. Several major media outlets are clamoring for a play-by-play. Russ Knocke will handle related calls.

15. Congressional investigation; Frist and Hastert announced a bipartisan "bicamera" committee to fully investigate the events surrounding local, state and federal response to Hurricane Katrina—to be completed by Feb 2006.

16. $58 billion supplemental request; President Bush requested an additional $58 billion in supplemental funding from Congress for hurricane relief and recovery.

17. National Day of Prayer and Remembrance; President Bush today named Friday, Sept. 16, 2005 a national day of prayer and remembrance to honor the victims and survivors of hurricane Katrina.

* * *

From: Bahamonde, Marty
Sent: Tuesday, September 13, 2005 4:33 PM
To: Taylor, Cindy
FW: Slowness of recovery of Katrina dead criticized
-----Original Message-----
From: Bahamonde, Marty
Sent: Tuesday, September 13, 2005 3:20 PM
To: Bergman, Cynthia; Knocke, William R; Besanceney, Brian
Cc: Rule, Natalie; Karonis, Jeff; Bahamonde, Marty
Subject: RE: Slowness of recovery of Katrina dead criticized

Admiral Allan Statement:

From the initial days following Hurricane Katrina, federal assets have worked closely with the State of Louisiana to help them implement their plan on retrieving the remains of those who perished. Federal agencies and the U.S. Military have brought in hundreds of resources to assist the state and have even sought outside resources to help them in the process. The State has always maintained direct control over the mortuary process following this tragedy. We are committed to a process that treats the victims of Katrina with dignity and respect, yet defer to State officials on what they believe to be the best solution for their constituents.

Any thoughts on this?

Marty

-----Original Message-----
From: Bergman, Cynthia
Sent: Tuesday, September 13, 2005 2:32 PM
To: Knocke, William R; Besanceney, Brian
Cc: Rule, Natalie; Karonis, Jeff; Bahamonde, Marty
Subject: Re: Slowness of recovery of Katrina dead criticized

Marty—what do you advise? Is the Gov willing to cooperate?

-----Original Message-----
From: Knocke, Russ
Sent: Tue Sep 13 15:11:40 2005
To: Karonis, Jeff; Bahamonde, Marty
Subject: Slowness of recovery of Katrina dead criticized

Cathy and Dana are suggesting a joint statement with the State, or even a conference call with the state. Please advise. Thanks . . . Russ

* * *

Slowness of Recovery of Katrina Dead Criticized

BATON ROUGE, Sept 13 (Reuters)—Louisiana's governor condemned the Federal Emergency Management Agency on Tuesday for moving too slowly to recover the dead from New Orleans and has signed a contract directly on behalf of the state with the recovery company originally hired by FEMA.

"I have taken action today to resolve a matter that involves life, death and dignity," Kathleen Blanco told reporters at a meeting of state elected officials. "I cannot stand by while this vital operation is not being handled appropriately."

Blanco said she has signed a contract with Kenyon International Emergency Services after the company threatened to pull out of the state because it had not yet signed a formal contract with FEMA.

Asked about the issue, FEMA spokesman David Passey said: "From what I understand, Kenyon had some questions about the contract."

He said from the beginning FEMA had expected Louisiana to take the lead in the collection of bodies and FEMA was satisfied that the state had signed a contract with the company.

"I don't know the exact nature of the contract concerns. We made our best effort to engage Kenyon in a contract," he said.

The fact that the state had signed a contract with Kenyon would allow federal mortuary teams to "get on with what they do best," the identification of the dead.

Blanco did not give details of the financial arrangements of the state's contract with Kenyon, and spokespeople for the company were not immediately available to comment.

Kenyon said on Sept. 7 it had been hired by FEMA for recovery services. FEMA has become the target of strong criticism of the Bush administration's handling of the hurricane, which struck the U.S. Gulf coast two weeks ago, killing hundreds and displacing 1 million people in the nation's worst natural disaster.

FEMA director Michael Brown, whose work was initially praised by President George W. Bush, resigned on Monday.

Bush himself took responsibility on Tuesday for failures in the federal response to Hurricane Katrina and acknowledged the storm exposed serious deficiencies at all levels of government four years after the Sept. 11 attacks.

Russ Knocke
Press Secretary
Department of Homeland Security

* * *

From: Rule, Natalie
Sent: Tuesday, September 13, 2005 6:05 PM
To: Kinerney, Eugene
Cc: Bahamonde, Marty; Taylor, Cindy
Subject: FW: FEMA order

Butch: This reporter just called asking for a response to the fact that the
Keith Ellison, southern district of Texas, just hosted a conference call at 4
p.m. today and said he would consider holding FEMA in contempt as we
have had more than enough time—as the federal coordination entity—to let
all parties know that they cannot block media from filming the body retrieval.
Apparently after this judge provided a temporary restraining order (issued
Saturday) allowing media to cover what they need, CNN came back and
complained that they are still being blocked by National Guard and others.
So they complained, and this conference call took place.

I think you have worked on this issue so far . . . guess we need to be quite
careful now that is a lawsuit. Who from OGC [Office of General Counsel]
do we need to bring in?

* * *

*And then the lawsuit began as the news media worked to be
allowed unlimited access in areas where we felt their presence
would be hurtful and the images would not add to the story
when the devastation and deaths were already well covered.
No family needed to see the partial remains of a loved one on
network television or on the front page of a newspaper. But our
perceptions of what the survivors were and would be enduring
did not matter. The media went to the courts.*

* * *

IN THE UNITED STATES DISTRICT COURT
FOR THE SOUTHERN DISTRICT OF TEXAS
HOUSTON DIVISION
CABLE NEWS NETWORK LP, LLLP, AND MICHAEL CARY
Plaintiffs,

v.

MICHAEL D. BROWN, in his capacity as Under Secretary
of Homeland Security for Emergency Preparedness and Response, and
Director of the FEDERAL EMERGENCY MANAGEMENT AGENCY,
Defendants.

ORDER GRANTING PLAINTIFFS' APPLICATION FOR TEMPORARY
RESTRAINING ORDER AND APPLICATION FOR INJUNCTIVE
RELIEF

Plaintiffs Cable News Network L.P., LLLP and Michael Cary in this
cause have filed a Verified Complaint, Application for Temporary Restraining Order and Application for Injunctive Relief and in connection
therewith have presented a request for a temporary restraining order as
set forth in their Complaint.

The Court hereby finds, that unless Defendants are immediately
restrained from the acts set forth below, Plaintiffs' First Amendment
right to be free of prior restraint and its First Amendment and common
law rights to access will be denied and the result will be an impermis-
sible prior restraint on publication on the basis of content:

Defendants and their agents have declared to Plaintiff that no
press coverage will be allowed during recovery of the deceased
victims of Hurricane Katrina.

The Court finds that if the commission of these acts is not restrained immediately, Plaintiffs will suffer irreparable harm and injury
because they will be denied their constitutional right of access to news,
information and images of the deceased victims' recovery efforts in
the hurricane disaster, and access to gather news, information and
images concerning the operations and activities of government. The

government's efforts also constitute an unconstitutional prior restraint and that Plaintiffs' and the general public's interests will be irreparably harmed because the governments operations and activities will be conducted in secret.

The Court hereby finds that immediate and irreparable injury, loss and harm will result to Plaintiffs in that Defendants have represented that the ban would become effectively immediately.

The Court finds that Plaintiffs have no adequate remedy at law because if not restrained, Plaintiffs will be denied access to what is going on in the deceased victims' recovery efforts as it is transpiring and likewise will be restrained from reporting on same.

For the foregoing reasons and the reasons set forth in the Complaint and Application for Temporary Restraining Order, the Court enters the following order.

IT IS HEREBY ORDERED that Defendants, their agents and anyone acting in concert with them are hereby commanded forthwith to refrain from or affirmatively permitting:

> Threatening action or taking any action to bar, impede or prevent Plaintiffs from their newsgathering and reporting activities in connection with the deceased hurricane Katrina victims' recovery efforts, including access to the sites, photographing or reporting.

IT IS FURTHER ORDERED that Defendants, their agents. and anyone acting in concert with them cease, desist and refrain from engaging in the conduct and activities described above from the date of the Order until 10 days after entry of the Order or until further order of this Court, whichever comes first.

IT IS FURTHER ORDERED that Defendants appear before the Court on _____ at _____ o'clock ___.m. in the Courtroom of _____, then and there to show cause why a temporary injunction should not be issued to Plaintiffs.

The Court finds that no bond is required.

SIGNED THIS _____ day of September, 2005, at _____ o'clock __.m

_____

JUDGE PRESIDING

* * *

Sent: Tuesday, September 13, 2005 7:28 PM
To: Bahamonde, Marty; Rule, Natalie
Re: Statement on photos of recovery supposedly from Allen

To: Hurricane Katrina Operations Personnel
Subject: Dignified Recovery of Human Remains
    1) Ensuring the dignified recovery of remains of those who lost their lives in the devastating tragedy is of critical importance.
    2) Although the media will not be embedded with Hurricane Katrina Operations, the media may be in the vicinity of a recovery operation and may endeavor to cover this mission. Thus, interaction between Hurricane Katrina Operations personnel and the media may result. Hurricane Katrina Operations personnel must be sensitive to the importance of ensuring a dignified recovery. If the media are in the vicinity of a recovery operation, they will be permitted to observe the operation from public property at a reasonable distance outside of the house, business or other structure in which the recovery operation is taking place. Media access will be addressed in cooperation with local authorities and consistent with the safety of all persons and the security and dignity of the operation.

* * *

From: Kinerney, Eugene
Sent: Tuesday, September 13, 2005 7:52 PM
To: Rice, Harvey
Cc: Rule, Natalie
Subject: RE: no luck reaching FEMA
Importance: High

Just for the record:

FEMA never issued any guidance, order, directive, rule or any other official communication regarding any photography or videography of the deceased. There was one comment made to one reporter by a FEMA employee which was taken out of context and which was interpreted by some to mean that we were restricting photography of the dead. FEMA's policy has always been that the dignity of the deceased is of the highest priority and that news organizations should use their judgment when deciding to photograph or publish images of bodies. That policy is made out of respect for the dead and their next of kin.

APPENDIX 2

WITH TIME COMES UNDERSTANDING

AFTER LEAVING government service I was interviewed many times about my work and my thinking. The following are statements made at that time. They accurately reflect my feelings following my experience with Katrina and the other disasters for which I coordinated response, as well as about the job that will be filled by other men and women in future administrations.

* * *

During my tenure as FEMA director I always dealt directly with the White House regarding natural disasters. In fact, the Department of Homeland Security was so disinterested in natural or manmade disasters that during Secretary Ridge's tenure he never participated in any disasters during the initial response phase, which, of course, is the most crucial as it focuses on lifesaving and rescue efforts. Only after the initial phase was over, and with approval of the White House, would Secretary Ridge enter a disaster area. For example, during the *Columbia* space shuttle disaster, Secretary Ridge did not enter the disaster area at all. During the California wildfires, he visited California after the President's visit, and only after the fires were under control. During the 2004 election while four hurricanes roared through Florida, Secretary Ridge came to Florida only after the White House approved a visit by him and HHS Secretary Tommy Thompson.

I do not recall Secretary Ridge ever calling or interfering with operations. He would call occasionally to offer moral support or to compliment the FEMA team on the job they were doing, but he never interfered with any operations. The White House, throughout each of these disasters, dealt directly with me. The President, and his White House staff, were always in direct contact with me regarding the situation "on the ground" and offered to do anything I needed for support.

There was never any question in my mind that I should deal directly with the White House until just days before I was removed from the Katrina operations by Secretary Chertoff, when White House chief of staff Andy Card told me in a telephone call that I should start going through the "chain of command," whatever that meant.

If I had to deal with the White House through Secretary Chertoff (or any other secretary, for that matter) it would have added another layer of bureaucracy, another step, when minutes made a difference between life and death. Readers should note that not only was it protocol for me to deal directly with the White House, but I often, with the support and approval (it was just the natural way to work) of the White House, dealt directly with other cabinet secretaries.

Common sense dictates this. You can call directly and speak to the "person in charge" (i.e., the President) or you can call an intermediary and wait for the transfer of information.

I should note that this was not an unusual practice, but a common one. James Lee Witt, under President Clinton, and Joe Allbaugh, under President Bush, always dealt directly with the President, even though they did not have a DHS secretary at the time. General Becton, FEMA director under President Reagan, has commented to Knight Ridder newspapers that not only does he believe the FEMA director should report directly to the President, he believes it is the director's obligation.

FEMA was at one time an "honest broker" among federal agencies. Since its inclusion in the Department of Homeland Security it has lost much of its ability to act as an honest broker.

Look at the practical side. DHS has a primary mission: to *prevent* acts of terrorism. This is clearly shown not only in the Homeland

Security Act but by the facts. With over 180,000 employees, more than 178,000 of those employees are engaged, in one way or another, with preventing acts of terrorism or performing law enforcement functions: Immigrations & Custom Enforcement, Customs & Border Protection, Secret Service, U.S. Coast Guard, Transportation Security Administration, and so on.

Only one agency, with only twenty-five hundred employees (or less right now because employees are leaving in droves), is responsible for *responding* to acts of terrorism or natural or manmade disasters: FEMA. Thus, the natural tendency within our form of government is to follow the money. That money is going toward crisis management, or law enforcement, instead of consequence management, or response. While DHS claims to be an all-hazards department (responding to all types of disasters) it is only lip service. Its primary function, funding, culture, and mission is to prevent terrorism—a worthwhile and necessary mission, but one that should not be to the detriment of disaster response.

INDEX

GUILDERLAND PUBLIC LIBRARY
2228 WESTERN AVENUE
GUILDERLAND, NY 12084-9701